THE TRUE STORY OF
ANDERSONVILLE PRISON

A DEFENSE OF MAJOR HENRY WIRZ

JAMES MADISON PAGE
2d Lieutenant Company A, Sixth Michigan Cavalry

THE TRUE STORY OF ANDERSONVILLE PRISON

A DEFENSE OF MAJOR HENRY WIRZ

By

JAMES MADISON PAGE

Late 2d Lieut. Company A, Sixth Michigan Cavalry

In Collaboration With

M. J. HALEY

With Portraits

New York and Washington
THE NEALE PUBLISHING COMPANY
1908

THE TRUE STORY OF
ANDERSONVILLE PRISON

By JAMES MADISON PAGE

A 1999 digital reproduction retaining the look and feel of the original work

Originally Published in 1908.
The Werner Company

For more information contact the publisher:
Digital Scanning, Inc.
344 Gannett Road, No. Scituate, MA 02066
http://www.digitalscanning.com

CONTENTS

PART I

ANDERSONVILLE: THE PRISONERS AND THEIR KEEPER

Chapter   I. MY FIRST SOLDIERING   15-24

My home and parents – my enlistment – I become a commissary-sergeant – We go after
Mosby – A matter of gallantry.

Chapter   II. A SPRINT AND A CAPTURE   25-40

Under the first fire – Snicker's Gap – The battle
of Falling Waters – We attack Hill's corps – A
good run – Taken prisoner.

Chapter   III. A PRISONER AT BELLE ISLE   41-52

Talk of immediate exchange – Eleven comrades – My illness – One red apple – "Market
street" – Billy Bowles's Christmas bill of fare.

Chapter   IV. FROM BELLE ISLE TO ANDERSONVILLE . .   53-58

The attitude of our jailers – We reach Andersonville – The camp and the stockade – The
site of the famous prison – "The knitting
women."

Chapter   V. DAILY LIFE AT ANDERSONVILLE   69-84

Building our cabin – The Twenty-fifth Alabama – A box from home – A cake of soap –
Winder takes command of Andersonville – I
meet Captain Wirz – His willingness to help
the prisoners.

Contents

6

Chapter   VI. THE DEAD-LINE AND THE DEATH OF
                "POLL PARROT"   85-98

Our cabin in danger – Captain Wirz's kindness – The "poisoned vaccine" – We build a
tunnel – "Poll Parrot" is suspected of being a
traitor – The duty of a sentry.

Chapter   VII. THE STANTON POLICY   99-109

Religious services – Captain Wirz makes corn
beer – No exchange – Despair – Secretary Stanton's theory of war.

Chapter   VIII. EXECUTION OF THE RAIDERS   110-125

The raiders at work – Captain Wirz aids the
prisoners – The execution of six of the raiders.

Chapter   IX. THE MASS MEETING OF JULY TWENTIETH   126-139

An over-crowded camp – Captain Wirz's sympathy with the prisoners – A meeting to urge
exchange – The resolutions and the committee –
"Little Red Cap" – Wirz and the drummer-
boys – Wirz pleads for better rations for the
prisoners.

Chapter   X. THE FATE OF A TRAITOR 140-146

A freshwater spring – Another tunnel – Another
discovery – The man who told.

Chapter   XI. THAT TERRIBLE AUGUST   147-163

Absence of Captain Wirz on a   furlough – The
death rate – Corn beer, a health beverage – The
results of a false war policy.

Chapter   XII. BILLY BOWLES GIVES A DINNER IN
                 BALTIMORE   164-180

Leaving Andersonville – Two out of eleven –
Millen prison – I become a shoemaker – My
new   clothes – The stars and   stripes – "What
beasts men are!" – At   Baltimore – Two out of
eleven – "Turn down an empty glass."

PART II

HENRY WIRZ: THE MAN AND HIS TRIAL.

Chapter   I. THE FACTS OF WIRZ'S LIFE 183-189

His parentage and education – His career as a
soldier – His foreign mission – The last dinner
with his family – The arrest and journey to
Washington.

Chapter   II. THE ACCUSATION AGAINST WIRZ 190-204

Special military commission – The specifications – The prisoner's plea.

Chapter   III. THE TRIAL   205-216

The banner witness, Felix de la Baume – Wirz
in the court-room – The charge of "conspiracy" – The findings of the commission – The
sentence.

Chapter   IV. THE LAST DAYS OF WIRZ'S LIFE 217-233

He is visited by Father Boyle – The newspaper gossip – Father Boyle's letter to Jefferson
Davis – An extract from the Confederate Veteran – Wirz's letter to Attorney Schade – Wirz's
letter to President Johnson – The New York
News correspondence – The execution.

Chapter   V. WIRZ'S ATTORNEY'S FINAL WORD 234-242

Attorney Schade's letter to the American public – "A friendless and forsaken man" – "We
cannot escape history."

Chapter   VI. THE GREAT WAR SECRETARY 243-248

The Character of Stanton – Conclusion – "One
people, one country, one flag."

PREFACE

During the past forty years I have read a number of stories of Andersonville Prison and of Major Wirz, who had subordinate charge of the prisoners there. Nearly all these histories were written by comrades who were confined there as prisoners of war. I do not propose in this work to question the accuracy of their portrayal of the great suffering, privations, and of the mortality of prisoners of war in Andersonville, for these are matters of fact that any one who was confined there can readily corroborate and can never forget. But it has been painful to me since the day I marched from that dismal prison pen, September 20, 1864, to the present time, that my comrades who suffered there and who have written their experiences are to a man wild in their charges that Major Wirz was responsible and that he was the sole cause of the suffering and mortality endured at Andersonville.

I have finally concluded to write something of my experiences in Southern prisons during the Civil War, not in a spirit of controversy, but in the interest of truth and fair play.

I was a prisoner in different places in the South

from September 21, 1863, till November 21, 1864, seven months of which I was at Andersonville.

The story of Andersonville has been already too often written for the mutual welfare of North and South, for the story as written has tended to increase the friction between the two great sections of our country. This is to be deplored, since every lover of his country desires, to the extent of his power, to allay all sectional bitterness.

The main purpose of the writer of this book is to reduce the friction between the two sections opposed to each other in the Civil War, and especially that caused by the exaggerated and often unjust reports of Major Wirz's cruelty and inhumanity to the Union prisoners, reports throughout the North at least, which have been represented to be gratuitous and wilful.

I am writing, not for the purpose of contradicting any comrade who has written before me, but to take a like liberty and to tell the story again from the standpoint of my own personal experience.

Taps will soon sound for us all who passed through those experiences, and I am sure that I shall feel better satisfied, as I pass down to the valley of death, if I say what I can truthfully say in defense of the man who befriended me when I was in the greatest extremity, and when there was no other recourse.

At the close of the war the feeling was so intense in the North on account of the suffering and mortality among the prisoners of war at Andersonville that something had to be done to satisfy the popular demand for the punishment of those supposed to be responsible for that suffering and the loss, of life among the prisoners, and Major Wirz was doomed, before he was tried, as the party responsible for these results.

In my prison life of seven months at Andersonville I became well acquainted with Major Wirz, or Captain Wirz, as he then ranked, and as he will hereafter be designated.

The knowledge I gained of his character during this personal acquaintance leads me to disagree with the conclusions reached by other writers as to the true character of this unfortunate man. During all these years it has been a matter of surprise to me that writers like Richardson, Spencer, Urban, and others failed to take into consideration the fact that Captain Wirz was but a subordinate under Gen. John H. Winder, who was the prison commander. Captain Wirz had charge only of the interior of the stockade, and in every way he was subject to the orders of his superior officer.

Nearly all these writers were soldiers, and should have known that obedience to superiors was imperative, and hence if there were fault or error in orders or in their execution it was to be charged against the superior and not the subordinate.

In this work I shall take the stand not only that

Captain Wirz was unjustly held responsible for the hardship and mortality of Andersonville, but that the Federal authorities must share the blame for these things with the Confederate, since they well knew the inability of the Confederates to meet the reasonable wants of their prisoners of war, as they lacked a supply of their own needs, and since the Federal authorities failed to exercise a humane policy in the exchange of those captured in battle.

The reader may expect in this account only the plain, unvarnished tale of a soldier. The writer, "with malice toward none and charity for all," denies conscious prejudice, and makes the sincere endeavor to put himself in the other fellow's place and make such a statement of the matter in hand as will satisfy all lovers of truth and justice.

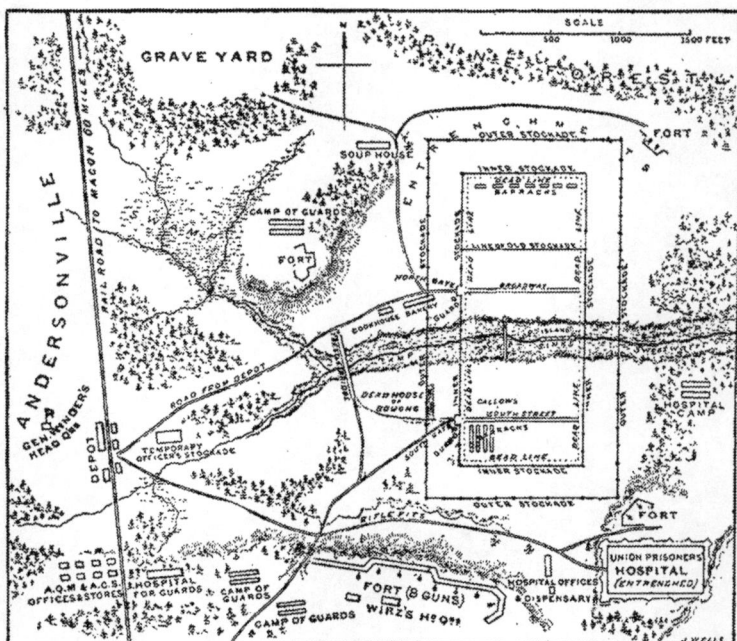

[From a sketch made in August, 1864.]

PLAN OF STOCKADE AND SURROUNDS AT ANDERSONVILLE

The outlines of the forts represented in the above cut differ from those on the opposite page, which are correct, owing to the fact that the person who made the sketch was not allowed to approach the forts.

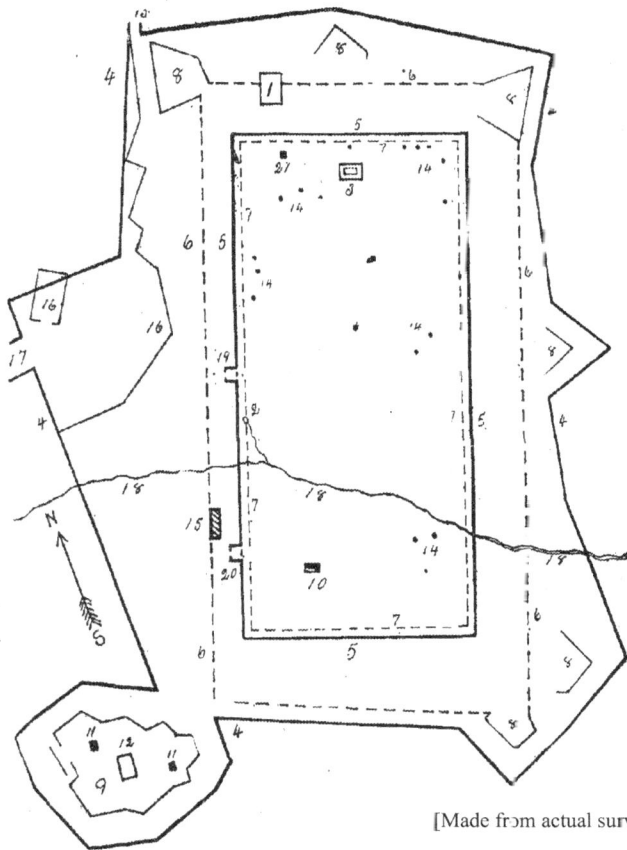

[Made from actual survey.]

PLAT OF ANDERSONVILLE PRISON GROUNDS

DESCRIPTION: 1 Care-taker's House, erected by the National W. R. C. 2 "Providence Spring" 3 Site of proposed National Monument. 4 Outline of purchased property. 5 Outline of Stockade enclosing prisoners. 6 Outline of Outer Stockade (only partially completed). 7 "Dead Line." 8 Confederate Forts and Batteries. 9 Main Fort of "Star Fort" southwest corner. 10 Site of Gallows, where marauders were hung 11 Powder magazines in "Star Fort." 12 Site of Capt. Wirtz' Headquarters. 13 Gate to roadway leading to the cemetary. 14 Wells and Tunnels dug by prisoners. 15 Site of Dead House. 16 Entrenched Camp for guards. 17 Roadway, 100 feet wide, leading to railroad station. 18 "Stockade Creek," a branch of Sweetwater. 19 North Gate of Stockade. 20 South Gate of Stockade. 21 Flag Staff.

PART I

ANDERSONVILLE: THE PRISONERS
AND THEIR KEEPER

W. J. W. Kerr, M.D.

CHAPTER I

MY FIRST SOLDIERING

I was born in Crawford County, Pennsylvania, July 22, 1839, the youngest of the five children of Wallace and Nancy Bonney Page. My parents were natives of Massachusetts, the former born in 1810 and the latter in 1816, and they were married on April 18, 1832, at Ellington, Chautauqua County, New York. My father's paternal grandfather was a soldier in the War of the Revolution, and the maternal grandfather of my mother was a soldier at the same time. Both were "Continentals" in the "Massachusetts Line," and both were honorably mustered out of service, a matter that has been a source of pardonable pride to their descendants.

The reader will pardon me for intruding these facts and also some succeeding ones relating to my ancestors and their descendants, but my purpose is to show how thoroughly "Yankee" I am in ancestry, birth, education, and environment. I never was as far south as Pittsburg, Pennsylvania, until I was a Union soldier on my way South.

My parents had five children: Elvira, Wallace Robert, Elmina, Rodney Walter, and myself, I being the youngest. We are all living, and have been for years residents of Pageville, Madison County, Montana.

In 1840 my father died when I was but one year old, and when I was thirteen my good mother died.

Soon after my father's death we removed to Michigan, where I received a good common school education and later I took a course at Eastman's business college at Chicago. I had a keen taste for mathematics, and would at any time much rather encounter the most difficult problem in trigonometry than place myself between the handles of a plow.

When the war broke out in 1861 I was engaged in extending the public surveys in northwestern Minnesota, east of the now flourishing city of Morehead. At that time that portion of our Uncle-Samuel-land was "way out west," and as the region was sparsely settled I was very busy. My calling was a lucrative one, and being far from "the bustling throng and the busy haunts of men" I scarcely heard anything about the "impending conflict."

I was incredulous relative to the threatened "clash of arms." I had been so surfeited with the inflammatory war talk emanating from both North and South that I was disgusted. I regarded almost anything more likely to happen than actual war between the two great sections of our country.

As late as 1861 I little thought that the greatest

war of history was to deluge our country with blood. Little did I think there would be calls by President Lincoln for soldiers ranging from 300,-000 to 500,000 each, and little did I think that rivers of blood would flow through our land and that half the homes, both North and South, would be in mourning ere the great strife would cease.

I gave the matter little thought until the great disaster that befell the Federal forces under General McDowell at the first battle of Bull Run on July 21, 1861. It could plainly be seen then that a gigantic struggle was at hand.

I was twenty-three when I enlisted in Company A, Sixth Regiment Michigan Cavalry, on August 14, 1862, at Grand Rapids, Mich., and was mustered into service August 28, 1862.

On December 10 the regiment proceeded to Washington, D. C., and went into camp on Meridian Hill between Seventh and Fourteenth streets. Our regiment was brigaded with the Fifth and Seventh Michigan Cavalry, and was attached to Casey's division of Weintzelman's corps. While at Washington I was promoted to commissary-sergeant.

During the winter of 1862-63 our regiment participated in several raids into Virginia, in one of which we went to Falmouth, where Burnside's army was encamped.

In the spring of 1863 the regiment broke camp at Washington and marched to Fairfax Court

2

House, and was kept on picket duty till June of
that year, Col. Geo. Gray commanding.

While on this duty the regiment often made
raids to the west of Fairfax, outside of our lines,
in quest of Colonel Mosby, who was continually
disturbing our peace of mind.

In my official but non-combatant capacity of
commissary-sergeant I had boyish, vague dreams
of capturing Mosby myself, and single-handed. I
could not think of anything that would more
readily change my chevrons to shoulder-straps.
Indeed, to be frank, I confess to a feeling of some
importance when I looked down and saw my
sleeves decked with commissary-sergeant's stripes,
and I felt the stirring of military ambition like that
of Napoleon's soldier who always carried a marshal's baton in his knapsack that he might be prepared to accept sudden promotion.

After we had become thoroughly conversant
with Mosby's dashing tactics we were not half so
anxious to capture him, and after forty odd years
cogitation I feel satisfied that perhaps it is just as
well that we didn't meet him at close range.

A number of incidents occurred while on these
raids that might be interesting, but I'll record only
one.

It was about the first of May, 1863, that Colonel Gray ordered the regiment ready to march
light. Early the next morning we started in the
direction of Winchester. It was understood that
we were this time really to bag Mosby and his

men, and the ambitious commissary-sergeant tem-
porarily took leave of his accounts and supplies
and rode with the fighting detachment. We picked
up two or three of Mosby's "raiders," and toward
noon we circled to the left and immediately passed
through a small hamlet on the Winchester pike.
In the edge of the town the regiment halted and
dismounted for noon rest, when Colonel Gray
called me and said, "Sergeant, did you notice that
large mansion standing well back of a magnificent
lawn, on our right a short distance back?" "Yes,
sir." "Well, you take two non-commissioned officers and twelve men, ride back there, station your
men around that house and adjacent buildings, and
give them instructions to shoot any one attempting
to escape that will not halt at a command, and
then go through that mansion from cellar to gar-
ret and seize anything contraband that you find."

Of all my duties as a soldier this was the one I
most detested.

I was soon on the ground and had stationed my
men. I felt like a trespasser when I approached
the door in company with Sergeant Parshall, whom
I asked to go with me in case of trouble. (Dick
Parshall was afterward one of Custer's best
scouts.) When I rang the bell the door was
opened by a fine-looking middle-aged woman, who,
upon hearing my business, was not slow in convey-
ing to me in language of scintillating scorn what
she thought of me and the whole Yankee nation.

In my placid answer to her furious arraignment

I said, "Madam, I am very sorry to disturb you
and I do not wonder that you are greatly distressed at this action, but I am acting under orders,
and if you knew how very disagreeable this task
is to me you would deliver to me at once the key
to every room in the house and facilitate the en-
joined search as much as possible." Thereupon
she reluctantly handed me a bunch of keys, and accompanied us to the third floor, where I made
short work of my search and returned to the second floor. In the second room I entered I found
three women, an unlooked-for find, and after a
hasty search of the apartment I excused myself as
gracefully as I could and retreated in good order.

Passing to another room on the same floor I
was surprised anew to find five ladies, as uncon-
cerned as though taking an afternoon tea and in-
dulging in gossip.

My curiosity was piqued. It was not probable
that these women all belonged to one household.
What common purpose, I queried, had drawn
them together?

I retreated again, and soon reached what
seemed to be a front-room parlor on the same floor.
The room was large, and well filled with some fifteen or twenty women. As soon as I recovered
from this, another shock of surprise, I said, "Ladies, I ask your pardon. I was not aware that
there was a convention of women assembled here
to-day, or I should have suffered arrest sooner
than to have disturbed you." They did not seem

to be in a humor to accept my apology, and the lady of the house, who was with me from the first, was joined by others of her pronounced opinions, and from this group of representative women I learned some things about myself and the Yankee army that I never knew before.

The sense of gallantry again overcame me, and I fell back before a superior force and was glad to retire from the unequal conflict.

I completed my search of the lower floor of the house as rapidly as possible. When I reached the front door, in taking my leave of the premises I handed the keys back to the mistress of the mansion and said, "Madam, I am very sorry that in obeying orders I have been the cause of so much annoyance to you, especially considering the unusual condition of your household."

I was about to bid her a respectful adieu, when I noticed a door at my right leading into a room some twelve by fifteen feet enclosing a portion of the porch. It had the appearance of having been built for a special secret purpose. Of course my duty required me to examine this room, and on finding it locked I asked for the key.

I shall never forget the look of consternation on the mistress's face upon my making this demand. This spirited woman, who during this short interview had steadily manifested a spirit of proud defiance, expressed in her entire disparagement of the Yankee army and myself in particular, was now overcome with apprehension and alarm, which were manifest in her suddenly changed bearing.

She very reluctantly handed me the keys and turned away. During this time Parshall had gone to the opposite end of the porch and was talking to the guard. I finally unlocked the door, feeling sure that I should find some of Mosby's men, and, revolver in hand, I was prepared to meet them. What met my gaze was the climax of the day's surprises and explained those before encountered.

The room was filled to the height of six feet or more with choice articles of food, such as baked turkey, chicken, hams, bread, pastry and the like, disposed tastefully in tiers, one above another.

For a brief moment I wistfully surveyed this tempting array of choice food, so powerful in its appeal to a soldier's usually ravenous appetite. But as I reflected upon the choice treat prepared at great pains by the women, and upon the disappointment that would result from not being allowed to serve it, and hearing Parshall returning, I hastily locked the door and handed the key to the madam, who meanwhile had been anxiously watching me. I now bade her good-by, and signaled the guards to withdraw, and started down the walk. Almost immediately she was by my side, and said in a trembling voice, "I owe you an apology. I have often said there was not a gentleman in the Yankee army, but I must except one. You have placed me, with my neighbors and friends, many of whom you have just seen, under great obligation. My heart sank when you insisted on going into that room. I fully expected you and your men would despoil us of the necessary food, prepared at great pains from our meagre resources. Imagine then my surprise when you locked the door so hastily for fear your comrade would see the contents of the room."

"Madam," I replied, "I thank you for your kind words, but I have only done my duty as I understand it. I am not in the army to increase the hardships of defenseless women. I assure you that I would gladly protect every one of them from the unnecessary hardships of this unfortunate strife. Their suffering is great — greater indeed than that of the men at the front, and is likely to increase as the war goes on."

This was a noble type of a Southern woman. She was particular to take my name, my company, and regiment, with the probable intent of making a definite record of this treatment, which she was pleased to regard as magnanimous. Months afterward, when suffering from hunger in Libby Prison and Belle Isle, I wished that I had taken *her address,* so, that I might have sent to her for a loaf of bread or half a chicken such as I saw in her home once, for I believe it would have been forthcoming had it been in her power.

She gave me a cordial hand shake and a "God bless you" when we parted, which touched me deeply.

After joining my company and making my report to the Colonel, an irrepressible curiosity on the part of Dick Parshall prompted him to inquire about some of the late proceedings of this incident that were mysterious to him. For instance, he asked, "What in thunder did you and the madam find to talk about so long? I began to fear that she had captured you." "She did," I answered. "Well, how did it happen?" he rejoined. "She appeared to take to you at the last to beat all. How did you manage it?" "By treating her and her friends as you and I would like to have our mothers and sisters treated under like circumstances," I replied. Again Dick broke out, "Say, old man, what did you find in that room on the porch? I was about to take a peep in there when you so suddenly closed and locked the door." "I will tell you some time, Dick, but not now," I replied.

After several days I let out the secret, and the boys laid it up against me as a special grievance that I did not give them the tip; for besides enjoying a luscious feast themselves, it would have been a good joke to beat Mosby and his men out of it.

CHAPTER II

Our regiment moved from Fairfax Court House on June 25, 1863, and when Hooker's army began its movement to intercept Lee, Stahl's division of cavalry was made a part of the Army of the Potomac at Edward's Ferry.

Kilpatrick succeeded Stahl in the command of the cavalry division and Col. Geo. A. Custer was promoted to the rank of brigadier-general from the rank of captain on Pleasanton's staff, and took Copeland's place in command of the Michigan Brigade, consisting of the First, Fifth, Sixth and Seventh Michigan Cavalry regiments. General Custer was first seen by us at the battle of Hanover, Pennsylvania, June 30, 1863, which was the first time that the Sixth, our regiment, was under fire, except on the skirmish line at long range. At the battle of Gettysburg General Custer ordered Captain Thompson, of my company, to charge Gen. Wade Hampton's cavalry in a narrow lane on the eve of July 2, the second day of the fight.

A most desperate hand-to-hand conflict ensued. We went into this charge 77 men, rank and file, and next morning my company could rally but 26. In less than one-half hour we lost in killed, wounded, and captured, 51 men. Captain Thompson was wounded, and S. H. Ballard, our second lieutenant, whose horse was shot under him, was captured, and remained a prisoner to the close of the war. I received a slight saber cut on the head, but, strange as it may seem, I knew nothing about it until the next morning, when on being awakened from a few hours' sleep I felt a peculiar smarting sensation on my head and found my hair matted with blood. A thorough washing revealed a slight cut on the top of my head, a wound about two inches long and only deep enough to draw blood. During "piping times of peace" at home it would have been considered quite a wound and I would have had the neighbors taking turns to look at it; but on the field of Gettysburg I would be laughed at for my pains if I showed it to any one, and I don't remember of any one knowing anything about it but myself. Moreover, under the burning sun of that 3d of July it bothered me considerably, but I did not report it to the surgeons. We were too busy fighting the "Johnnies."

On July 4, at 10 a. m., our division being in advance, we marched from the sanguinary field of Gettysburg to intercept the enemy, who was retreating along the South Mountain road toward Williamsport. We marched by way of Emmettsburg up the road to Monterey, a small place as it appeared at night on the top of South Mountain range. On the 5th of July we had some skirmishing with the enemy's cavalry, and encamped that night at Boonsboro, Maryland.

On the 8th our regiment had an engagement with the enemy's cavalry on the Hagerstown road near Boonsboro, and three of our company were wounded. We were also engaged July 11, 12, 14, 20 and 24.

On July 14 our regiment was sharply engaged at the battle of Falling Waters, and had a number killed and wounded. Among the killed of the Sixth Michigan Cavalry were Capt. David G. Boyce and Maj. Peter A. Webber. I may be pardoned, perhaps, in quoting what was said about our brigade at this battle, and particularly of the Sixth Michigan Cavalry, of which I was a member. The *New York Herald* contained the following:

"Hearing that a force had marched toward Falling Waters, General Kilpatrick ordered an advance to that place. Through some mistake, only one brigade, that of General Custer, obeyed the order. When within less than a mile of Falling Water the enemy was found in great numbers and strongly entrenched behind a dozen crescent-shaped earthworks. The Sixth Michigan Cavalry was in advance. They did not wait for orders, but one squadron, Companies C and D, under Captain Boyce (who was killed), with Companies B and F, led by Major Webber (who was killed), made the charge, capturing the works and defenders. It was a fearful struggle, the rebels fighting like demons. Of the 110 men engaged on our side, but 30 escaped uninjured. This is cavalry fighting, the superior of which the world never saw."

On this campaign our regiment had a strenuous time of it. For seventeen days and nights we did not unsaddle our horses except to readjust the saddle-blankets.

The next trouble we had was when we crossed the Potomac into Virginia in the rear of Lee's army and encountered Stuart's cavalry at Snicker's Gap, on July 19. The charge was simultaneous and I came near "passing in my checks," for I was knocked from my horse in the charge and was run over by half our regiment. I was stunned and badly bruised, but not cut. When I came to I was glad to find that my sore head was still on my shoulders. I was soon mounted, and our regiment went into camp.

We remained there next day awaiting rations, and, while riding from the quartermaster's tent to my company, I crossed a field that was overgrown with weeds and briers and ran against a gray granite slab. I dismounted, and pulling the briers aside, I saw that it was a gravestone. The inscription stated the man's name and age, which I have forgotten; the date of his death at an advanced age, in 1786, and concluded with this quaint inscription:

"Man, as you are passing by,
As you are now, so once was I;
As I am now, so you must be;
Turn to God and follow me."

This affected me deeply. The thought occurred to me that when in life (for he died but three years after the Revolution) how little he expected that the time would come when his beautiful domain and his bright sunny Southland would be devastated and laid waste by an invading army of his own countrymen!

From June 30 to September 21, 1863, our regiment participated in seventeen skirmishes and battles On September 14, at Culpeper Court House, General Custer was wounded and the command of the brigade devolved upon Colonel Sawyer of the First Vermont Cavalry, which was brigaded with us at the time.

On taking command Sawyer seemed to think that the war had been going on long enough, and he decided to end it at once. Like Pope, his headquarters were in the saddle. "Up and at them" was his motto. He wasn't, as yet, even a brigadier by brevet, but visions of the lone star on his shoulders, I presume, took possession of him. "Dismount and fight on foot!" was the ringing order from the Colonel on September 21, at Liberty Mills, on the Rapidan, and, as had been my habit, I snapped my horse to a set of fours of led horses, and borrowing the gun and cartridge-box of the soldier in charge of the horses, I joined my company commanded by

Capt. M. D. Birge. We crossed the bridge and deployed in a cornfield on the left of the road. I was on the extreme left, and paid very little attention to the regular line, as I was an independent skirmisher; but as soon as I found that more than twenty of us were separated from the line by drifting into an open ravine for better protection, I was a trifle tamer than when I started out a half hour previous. On the right the corn was cut and stood in shocks, and while the line advanced up the ravine I ascended the ridge, keeping under cover as well as I could behind the corn shocks. When I reached the top of the elevation I was completely staggered to see several hundred mounted Confederates advancing toward us, platoon front, as if on parade. There was no time to lose, for the lead was crashing through the shock that I was behind, at a fearful rate, and how I escaped with only a rip in my blouse near my left elbow is more than I shall ever know. I had possibly three hundred yards to run to reach the boys, now under command of Lieutenant Hoyt. I safely got where they were without being hit, but the time I made in doing so would have been creditable to the fleetest jack-rabbit.

I reported the danger we were in. All this time a mounted staff-officer a few hundred yards back of us was shouting himself hoarse, "Advance, men, advance!" "I cannot fall back when ordered to advance," said Hoyt. "Lieutenant, if you do not we are lost," was my reply. The soldier will at once realize the embarrassment of my position in advising a retreat. It savors so much of the "white feather." It is always well enough for the inferior to advise a forward movement, even though the superior ignores the advice, but it is a ticklish thing to advise retreat — even the word "retreat" is dangerous. I knew the danger, because I saw it. The ground was undulating, and neither Lieutenant Hoyt nor the frantic staff-officer could see the advancing body of Confederates. "We will be surrounded and scooped up in less than five minutes," said I. "I cannot help it," replied Hoyt, "I must obey orders. Forward!"

We advanced perhaps a dozen rods, when the enemy was upon us. A Minie ball struck Hoyt in the shoulder and he was down. The charge followed. We received no more bellowing orders from the elegantly attired staff-officer. He at once adopted Falstaff's advice about "discretion being the better part of valor," and the skirts of his beautiful dress-coat would have made tails for a kite. The speed with which he reached a safe rear was of the fleetest. I can imagine his report to Colonel Sawyer, commanding brigade. It ran something like this: "They were captured because they did not obey my orders. I remained as long as possible, but was obliged to fall back."

I tried to get Hoyt away, but he was so badly hurt that he begged to be left on the field. I then gave orders to our men to fall back as quickly as possible to the river. We all started on the run down the ravine. I certainly out-ran them, for I was the only one that reached the stream. I was pretty fleet of foot myself in those days. The Confederates were busy picking up our boys, and I think for a moment they lost sight of me. I crossed the river and hid in the tall grass, and from where I lay I could see our boys being marched up the hill through the cornfield under guard.

While I do not know it for certain, yet I am, and always have been, satisfied that at about the time Lieutenant Hoyt was hit the Confederate officer in command gave the order to cease firing. Our miserable little handful of men was as good as captured at any time after the Confederate advance had reached the brow of the hill, and here is a marked refutation of the oft-repeated "needless rebel cruelty." We were engaged in an open fight, and they could have wiped us off the face of the earth at any time after getting over the hill, for they were upon us. I was repeatedly ordered to halt after getting 300 or 400 feet start, and could easily have been shot down before I reached the river; but I didn't have time to halt or to obey orders. According to all the rules of war they were perfectly justified in killing me when I failed to stop.

This magnanimous trait is particularly conspicuous in the Southern soldier. He will fight, day or night, against superior odds, but on the other hand, when the advantage is greatly in his favor, he views the situation in altogether a different light. It seems as if the spirit of magnanimity overcomes him.

It always was, always has been, and always will be a matter of profound wonderment why Beauregard and Johnston did not march upon Washington during the night cf July 21-22, 1861. All that they had to do was to reach out and take the city.

But the Southerners did not have a monopoly altogether in chivalrous conduct toward the defeated. When Pickett made that awful charge on the Union lines at Gettysburg, and when his brave men were being mown down, falling, wavering, and about to fall back, knowing that they had failed, a young beardless Confederate color-bearer, in advance of the line, looking to the right and left and seeing his comrades reeling, dropping, and wavering, deliberately raised the colors high in the air and jabbed the staff into the ground. He stepped back a pace or two, straightened himself like an adjutant on parade, and seemed to say, "I think that I might as well die here," and folded his arms. The smoke cleared away. Firing had not ceased however. "Don't kill that boy! Don't fire at that boy!" yelled Col. P. P. Brown, of the One Hundred and Fifty-seventh New York Regiment.

The young hero was not 150 feet from the

3

Union line. His look of despair gave place to a smile. He put his hand to his cap in salute and the Union men cheered. Taking the colors he turned about and slowly followed his brave comrades. Not a solitary one of Pickett's heroes was behind him except the dead and dying.

It is recorded as an act of extraordinary bravery, that when Napoleon was making his disastrous retreat from Moscow, one day, when closely beset, Marshal Ney, who commanded the rear, ordered a captain to remain with his company and to protect the rear of the rear-guard. "How long will I remain?" inquired the captain, realizing the utter hopelessness of the position. "Until you are killed!" was the answer. "Very well, sir." The captain never was heard of after. He was not a whit braver than the young Confederate color-sergeant.

Well, there I lay, concealed in the grass, congratulating myself upon my lucky escape and wondering how it happened. Although slighted by Mars, the god of war, I had been greatly favored by Mercury, the speedy one. It looked as if he had a wing over me.

I fully expected our cavalry to advance in force, and I thought that if I could manage to conceal myself for a little while I would soon be among my friends. But in this I was doomed to disappointment, for instead of the main body of our force putting in an appearance, a troop of Confederate cavalry crossed the river to bait their horses about where I lay, and to prepare their supper. A horse shied and snorted, and I was discovered and made a prisoner by a squad of the Fifth Virginia Cavalry.

"Why didn't you keep a-runnin'?" laughingly inquired a corporal in gray. He had seen me while I was sprinting riverward.

I had parched corn for supper. It was the best that my captors had, there was that consolation in it. While the rations were meager, our captors fared no better. I was kept under guard and treated with the utmost consideration. With the exception of that pleasant laughing "Why didn't you keep a-runnin'?" I didn't hear an insulting remark from those men.

Next morning I received an extra ear of parched corn, and was taken to the headquarters of Gen. A. P. Hill, guarded by four men in gray. The General asked me a number of questions, and his manner was so mild and genial that I began to think that it wasn't such a dreadful thing to be a prisoner.

I was then turned over to the provost marshal, and I learned that Colonel Sawyer had, in sending twenty-four of us in advance, actually attacked Gen. A. P. Hill's corps of 10,000 men. The great Southern general was very much amused over the incident, but for my humble part I could absolutely see nothing funny about it. I didn't enjoy it a particle.

I found myself in a camp of sixty-five or seventy

men under a strong guard. They were nearly all
Confederate soldiers under arrest for desertion,
and were waiting for their turn to be court-martialed. From twelve to fifteen were tried each
week, and those found guilty were shot on Satur-
days. There were nine poor fellows who had
been tried and found guilty. These men were
confined in an adjacent camp. I do not think
there was a time from Tuesday, the day I reached
there, until Saturday, when I was sent to Richmond, that some of them were not praying and
singing, in view of their fate.

I looked about me, and am ashamed now to
confess that it was then with a feeling of regret
that I could not discover the doughty staff-officer
among us. He took care to make good his escape.

One afternoon a young fellow of about twenty-
one years of age was brought back to the camp
under guard after being sentenced to death. That
same evening he sang "The Bonnie Blue Flag."
His tenor voice was pitched at a high key and I
never heard a sweeter voice, nor, I might add, a
sadder one. Next day he was shot by his own
comrades-in-arms. I am naturally sympathetic,
and the sentence and death of this young fellow
affected me greatly. Afterward I saw men by
the hundreds dying about me at Belle Isle and Andersonville, affecting and harrowing sights; but
as there was no help for it, and as I had perhaps
become accustomed to misery, it didn't touch me

so keenly. But there was such an air of abandonment and recklessness about the young fellow, and I don't believe that from the time he was sentenced until he faced death he thought of uttering a prayer. I can never forget his last words to us, "Good-by, fellows; I am bound for the happy land of Jordan," and he turned toward us and smiled.

I did not learn what induced him to desert, but it certainly was not cowardice. It was said he was caught making his way to the Union lines.

Our camp, under guard, was situated in a beautiful grove of chestnut timber, and the first night I slept soundly, having had little rest for several preceding nights. Notwithstanding my weariness, I was awakened during the night by some one pushing me as if trying to turn me over. I sat up, and found one of the soldiers wearing the Federal uniform sitting close beside me. I had taken note of him the previous evening. "Am I in your way?" I inquired. "Oh, no," was the answer, "you are not in my way," and I laid down and fell asleep again. When I awoke in the morning I found that the pockets of my blouse and trousers were cut across and the contents, consisting of $20 in money, my watch, pocketknife, sundry papers, tobacco, and pipe were gone. I knew at once that it was the young fellow in blue that robbed me.

There were a number of North Carolina boys in camp, very decent fellows, who, were very indig-

nant upon seeing my clothing so badly cut. The
corporal of the guard asked me whom I suspected,
and I told him. He brought the fellow to me, and
when I accused him of the theft he denied it with
a great show of indignation, and made all manner of threats of what he would do to me if I did
not at once withdraw the charge. I realized that
I was — to borrow an expression of to-day — "up
against it," and I was about to drop the matter,
when I caught a very broad wink from the corporal who was standing behind the fellow, and I
saw that I had a friend "at court." "You have
every reason to believe," said the corporal, "that
this man stole your property?" "Yes, sir," I replied.

About this time the officer of the day appeared
on the scene. The corporal spoke to him in an un-
dertone, whereupon the officer had the young fellow searched, but nothing was found on him.
"I'll give you twenty minutes," said the officer,
"to get those articles and restore them to the prisoner." Then, instead of further denial, he became sullen and refused to move. The officer had
his men "buck and gag him," and he was left in
that condition for at least two hours. The officer
returned and released him, and again ordered him
to restore to me my property. "I'd see him and
you in hell first!" was the reply. The officer ordered his men to get a rope and the sergeant secured one. "I'll give you five minutes to get the
articles," was the order. But the fellow neither

moved nor uttered a word. "Sergeant, have a couple of your men string him up," was the next command. They put the rope around his neck and threw the end of it around an overhanging limb. "Haul away!" and he went up six or seven feet. "Lower away!" and he came down and landed on his feet gasping. "Now will you get the property?" said the officer, but he received no reply. I interposed, and begged that the matter be dropped, saying that my loss was nothing compared to taking the fellow's life. The officer said he didn't know about that, that unless he was very much mistaken his life was hardly worth saving. "Pull away!" he ordered, and up went the culprit once more. The young fellow must have been suspended, dangling, eight or ten seconds before the lieutenant ordered the men to lower him. I became frightened, thinking that the lieutenant was really in earnest. He struck the ground as limp as a sack, and when he recovered his speech he said that he would get the articles, and, staggering away, he soon returned with them. He had dug a hole in the ground under where he slept, and after burying the articles had covered the place over with leaves. I thanked the officer for the interest he had taken in the matter.

I relate the incident here to show how fair and honest these men were. I have read much about our prisoners being robbed of money, watches, jewelry, and clothing upon entering Libby, Belle Isle, Andersonville, Salisbury, and other prisons in the South, but as far as I personally was concerned, I can truthfully testify that neither at Libby, Belle Isle, Andersonville, nor Millen, where I was confined, were any articles taken from me. I had $20 when I entered Libby and Belle Isle, and $30 or $40 of Confederate money when I entered Andersonville, and not one penny was taken from me. The Confederate officers and men at Libby and Belle Isle also knew that I had a watch with me, for I made no secret of it. They did not demand. it of me, though it was a valuable timepiece.

CHAPTER III

A PRISONER AT BELLE ISLE

On the 25th day of September I was sent to Richmond, arriving there at night, and was soon in Libby Prison among my comrades of the skirmish line who had preceded me a few days. I now learned that Lieutenant Hoyt, after being kindly treated by his captors, had been paroled on account of his wounds and sent to Washington.

We were at Libby prison only three days, when we were sent under guard to Belle Isle.

The first prisoners sent to Belle Isle had been supplied with tents, but these were all occupied, and we were compelled to camp on the ground without shelter of any kind and without fire. The evenings, particularly, were cold and we were thinly clad. Some writers have steadfastly asserted that the Confederate authorities never furnished tents or any kind of shelter at Belle Isle. This is a mistake.

When we reached the island there were about 5,000 prisoners, of whom only one-fourth were without shelter. As we entered the camp the other prisoners crowded about us with the usual questions, "What regiment? When were you captured? What news have you? What is the prospect of exchange?"

"Exchange" was the sole topic. It was on every one's lips. It was discussed by the suffering men, to whom "exchange" meant all that they asked for in this world. It meant life, home, mother, wife, sweetheart, friends — everything.

I found a number of my regiment here, and they had been prisoners a long time. They informed me almost immediately that it was understood that they were to be exchanged in "a day or two."

It has been often laid up against the Southern officers and men guarding us as a grievous fault that they continually held out "false hope" of exchange, well knowing that they absolutely had no grounds for the statements, and that they would say that we were about to be exchanged when there was not the least expectation of it. I thought then and I think still that these were meritorious "white lies," similar to the profanity of my Uncle Toby in "Tristram Shandy," where the Recording Angel, after recording the oath, blotted it out with tears.

The hope of exchange, though deferred, often prolonged and saved the life of many a prisoner of war, both North and South. It was a well-known fact among prisoners, whether at Andersonville or Belle Isle, Rock Island or Elmira, that if once an inmate became discouraged and lost hope he was doomed. Nothing could save him.

"Yank, you are looking pretty pert this morning," a rebel officer or soldier would say, "so you mustn't get discouraged. Brace up; never say die. You will be exchanged in a few days. I have it straight from headquarters."

Looking back more than forty years and diagnosing those "rebel lies," I can find no better reason for them than kindness of heart. Others can form any opinion they please, but these are my conclusions.

The first day I was at Belle Isle a rebel guard gave me a sheet of paper and an envelope, and I wrote to Captain Birge of my company and sent it out by comrade Crawford of Company F of my regiment, who was listed for exchange. This letter was received and forwarded to my sister, Mrs. Henry Utley, now of this State. She has preserved this letter with others that I wrote while a prisoner and recently she loaned them to me. I have them before me now.

The letter that I particularly refer to is, in part, as follows:

"Camp Yankee, Belle Isle,
"Richmond, Virginia, September 28, 1863.

"Capt. M. D. Birge, Co. A, Sixth Mich. Cavalry.

"Dear Captain: Hoyt, Swain, Douglas, and myself, with nineteen of Company L, Seventh Cavalry, were taken prisoners on the left of cur line on the 21st inst. and here we are, with the exception of Hoyt, on Belle Isle. Hoyt was badly wounded and has been paroled and sent to Washington.

"Considering the scanty rations, the awfully exposed and shelterless condition of the prisoners, and the evident inability of the Confederate authorities to feed and shelter, even the guards, to say nothing of the constantly increasing number of prisoners, I cannot believe that our Government will permit us to remain here very long, so I fully expect to be with you soon. We are hoping and praying to be soon exchanged. Now is the time for the Government to act, for if the 4,000 or 5,000 men that are now here are held until the winter begins, what remains of them will be unfit for service the coming year, if ever."

The air was full of reports that we would be exchanged, and I fully believed it, for I felt that the Federal authorities were well aware of the impoverished condition of the Confederate States and the great suffering and mortality that would follow if the prisoners were held through the winter months. We were fully convinced that our Government would at once take action to save the lives of its soldiers suffering in prison; but in this we were doomed to disappointment. Looking back at it now, it seems incredible and monstrous that the Secretary of War could deliberately close his eyes and ears to our suffering and want. It was well for us that we could not foresee what was in store for us in the many long, terrible months to come, for if we had known, the strongest would have sank in despair. As it was, we were buoyed up with the hope and report that we would be exchanged "next week." That report was constantly afloat in the camp.

My experience on the island is as vivid in my memory as if it happened last week. I shall never forget it. There were eleven of us that stuck together and helped each other like brothers. While none of us had been deprived of anything that we had in our possession when captured, we were all short of overcoats or blankets, and the nights were cold and the ground damp and as hard as a pavement. Night after night I walked back and forth to keep warm, but toward morning would tumble over through exhaustion and fall asleep. In this way I contracted a severe cold and fell sick with fever. My boys secured a piece of canvas about six feet square, so part would be over and part under me, and before long they got possession of a tent that was left them by a few friends who, in some way, were exchanged. They took the best care of me possible without medicine. It was an utter impossibility to obtain medicine for love or money. For eight days and nights I lay there unconscious, continually calling for water, and when the fever left me I couldn't believe that I had been sick eight days until they showed me the eight pieces of corn bread, our daily rations, that, notwithstanding their short allowance and craving for food, they had saved for me. There was no doubt of the eight days, for there was the evidence. I well knew that there could be no surplus bread lying around loose. Bread was too scarce.

That day a sergeant of the guard visited me. He conveyed the glad but weather-beaten tidings of exchange, but not in the old stereotyped form this time. He said it would come "to-morrow." Blessings on him, if alive; and if dead, may the earth lie lightly upon him!

This time I was sure of it. I tried to get on my feet, but could not. Finally, after being helped to a standing position, supported by a comrade on each side and encouraged by the rebel's advice, "never say die," I managed to take a few steps, but my knees refused to act their part.

It would never do to have the boys leave me next day, I thought. They promised not to go without me. I thought the "to-morrow" would never come, but it did, and the next day, and the next and the next, and we were still on Belle Isle.

Just a word more about the cheerful and encouraging "exchange" rebel falsifier. I cannot think of him other than that of a pure philanthropist and humanitarian. We had no medicine and he had none to give us. We were his enemies invading his country. There was war, "grim-visaged war," between us, and he could have done a thousand times worse than to say, "You will be exchanged to-morrow." He could, with hard, cold truth have said to me, "You may not die just yet, but you might as well; and if you do it will be mighty small loss. It will be one enemy less; and, suppose you do not die just yet, your prospect is a tough one, for your Government is about to shut down the lid as far as exchanging prisoners is concerned, if it hasn't already, and you will be here and at Andersonville, where you won't even have corn bread to eat, for the next fourteen months." Had I known then what was in store for me I never could have survived Belle Isle.

"Allowing for the sake of argument," said the priest to Voltaire, "that you are right; that there is no God; that there is no eternity and no future reward for the good and no punishment for the wicked, and that death is the end of us, where does the benefit of your boasted 'enlightenment of the human race' come in? Does your doctrine improve matters? What do you give us in exchange for our faith and hope of future reward that we so firmly believe in?"

The priest had the philosopher, metaphorically speaking, on the hip.

I was very weak, but through the kindness. of my friends, who tenderly nursed me through my sickness, I was soon able to walk. It was nothing short of a miracle that I pulled through this sickness, and as I gained strength I became ravenously hungry. It seemed as if I was trying to make up for lost time and get even with my eight days' fast. The tears come to my eyes now when I recall the many instances of — I must call it deception, on the part of my comrades in order to divide their meager rations with me.

"Here, Jim," said Bowles, a few days after I had got on my feet, "take part of my hoe-cake and put it down your neck. I am not very hungry to-day and have had enough." He was starving and I knew it.

Oh, how tenderly they cared for me — Bowles and Whitcomb and Swain and Dalzell and Douglas and Monroe and Whitworth and Holcomb!

Thanks to the brave fellows, I gained strength and lived.

While I was convalescing, a rebel soldier off duty passed me one day with a bundle. He turned and keenly looked at me. I was little more than skin and bones. After eyeing me for a second with a look of "Southern hatred" and with an air of "studied cruelty," he handed me a large red apple, and adding insult to injury, he said, "Stick your teeth into that apple, Yank, and try for a minute to fohget about the Nawth."

He hurried away before I had time to thank him; in fact, he didn't give me an opportunity to speak a word. I was dumbfounded. His reward will come to him hereafter.

I never saw him afterward, although I tried to find him, and my seeming ingratitude has been a source of regret to me ever since. I hugged the apple to my breast, then sat down and cried. I then took it to the boys and insisted upon its being divided. "No," said Swain, "it will only be a taste for us. Don't be silly, Jim. You must eat it yourself." But it was passed around and each one took a good smell of it. It was one of those fine, large apples with a delicious fruity aroma.

I kept the apple until the following day, when one of our men happened to get a loaf of white bread. He gave me a liberal portion of it, and with half the apple, for I would have no more, I had a feast, and I thought that when I got home I never would want anything to eat but white bread and apples.

After this I fully recovered my health and strength, and soon entered into active business on "Market Street."

I sold my watch (a present from my brother Rodney) to one of the guards and laid out the price of it in a stock of salables, consisting of sausage, biscuits, chewing and smoking tobacco, and such things. Each day I would take a portion of my merchandise and prepare it for sale by retail. The sausage I cut into small pieces, and putting part of my stock as temptingly as I could on a piece of board, I marched up and down Market Street, which ran from the main entrance through the prison grounds, crying out my wares: "Here is your fresh, delicious sausage, only ten cents in money or a dollar in 'confed.' " My business was fairly good, but I was more than eating up the profits. I kept at it day after day, buying a fresh supply with the money I was taking in; but both stock and money were dwindling. At night I would be tired and would sleep well. In this way

4

I kept my mind occupied, and obtained a little means to satisfy my cravings for food, which helped me to endure my miserable surroundings.

At last I "went broke," and something had to be done to get back in business again. I made a bargain with one of the guards. I traded him a pair of expensive cavalry boots that cost me $15 shortly before I was captured, for a haversack full of small hard biscuits and a quantity of tobacco. As soon as I reached my tent I gave half my stock to Dar Swain, my bunk-mate. It was evening and I was very hungry, but I concluded to pass the night on an empty stomach rather than the next forenoon. I wanted to be in the best condition possible to re-embark in the mercantile business, and placed my stock in trade under my head for a pillow. Next morning my first thought was for my valued haversack, and I reached for it and found it missing. Some "Yank," hungrier than myself, had purloined it by cutting a hole in the tent. I don't think that I ever met with a loss in my life that I felt as keenly as this. But Swain had his share safe and another division was made of the property.

Eleven of us that were captured together, all close friends and comrades, now occupied an old bell tent that furnished us shelter. Our condition was far better than it had been before I was taken sick, and about the first of November blankets were issued to each one of us by the Confederate authorities. This was a God-send to the prisoners, as the weather was getting more severe.

Of the eleven, I can remember the names of nine, Wm. Bowles and T. T. Whitcomb of Company L, Sixth Michigan Cavalry. The others belonged to Company A, Sixth Michigan Cavalry, namely: Darwin P. Swain, Wm. Dalzell, Reuben B. Douglas, David A. Monroe, Wm. G. Whitworth, John Holcomb, and myself.

The liveliest one of our squad was Wm. V. Bowles, first sergeant of Company L, Sixth Michigan Cavalry. He was a natural-born soldier; born and reared in the English army, where his father was a soldier. He was a hardy, jolly companion, always making the best of everything and thankful that it was no worse; but on Christmas Day, when for some unknown cause there were no rations issued to us and we were obliged to retire to our quarters unusually hungry, it was too much for Bowles, and he lustily cursed the "blowsted" Southern Confederacy for giving him nothing to eat on Christmas Day.

"Why, ye knaw," said he, "the lowiest 'cottier' in England will have his roast beef and plum puddin' on Christmas Day!" He cursed the whole country from Baffin's Bay to the Gulf of Mexico. The Washington Government and Secretary Stanton came in for a full measure of vigorous profanity. He wound up with, "You half-starved Yankees, we are not going to be cheated out of our Christmas dinner. I shall now invite you all to a

Christmas dinner to take the place of this one that
we didn't have to-day. As soon as we are exchanged I shall set up the dinner and pay for it
myself." And, taking a small memorandum-book,
he took down our names and made out a bill of
fare. It was an elaborate menu. We expected as
usual to be exchanged in a few days.

Bowles's bill of fare was an inviting one. It
consisted, to begin with, of turkey stuffed with
oysters, plum pudding and roast beef. I have forgotten the minor items. We knew that he would
keep his word if he had to pawn his clothes. Bill
Bowles never went back on a friend and never went
back on his word.

The bill of fare was headed with: "Bill of fare
that we didn't get at Belle Isle, on Christmas,
1863." The discussion of this forthcoming dinner
brought tears to the eyes of the most of us, but
there was not that degree of grief that was exhibited by the very few of us who did really par-
take of that dinner, precisely as Bowles designed it,
after we were exchanged at Baltimore, late in
1864. Only two of us partook of it, but Sergeant
Bill Bowles kept his word.

CHAPTER IV

FROM BELLE ISLE TO ANDERSONVILLE

The preacher, God bless his memory! was in evidence at Belle Isle. His ministration was the most consoling, and the hymns were a grateful accompaniment of the word preached. While in youth my musical education was sadly neglected, and I did not soar any higher than the "Arkansas Traveler" or "There is a Low Green Valley on the Old Kentucky Shore." I was fond of vocal music of a non-classical character.

A soldier named Daniel Finch, belonging to an Illinois regiment, composed a song with "local coloring." It was a parody on "Ho, Bob Ridley, Ho." Dan was a good singer and could always collect a crowd. I can remember only the first few lines:

> "The Johnnie Reb is a funny man,
> He feeds us on the Southern plan.
> Our tent is open behind and before,
> And a 'grayback' guards us at the door.
> Ho, Belle Island, ho! and ho, Belle Island, ho!"

Our guards enjoyed Finch's song as much as we did, and he would sing it for them at the slightest request.

"Say, Dan, who told you that there was a door to a tent?" inquired one of the boys. "Oh, I know that a 'flap' would sound better, but I was bothered about the rhyme."

Dan Finch was one of those cheerful, obliging fellows who make friends on all sides. He was a born diplomat, and in January made himself one of the needles that the exchange manipulators found in the hay-stack. We didn't envy him his extraordinary good luck, for each individual one of us hoped that the case might soon be his own; but we sadly missed his smiling face and genial ways. I have forgotten, if I ever knew, whether he was exchanged or paroled. He was liked by rebel officers and guards, and they might have had something to do with selecting him for exchange. His Belle Isle song was humorous, and in no manner insulting or disrespectful to our "seceded brethren." It was the song of the politician, diplomatic in the extreme, and he was wise, knowing full well that the "rebs" had the drop on us. In one part of his poetical effusion he portrayed the "Johnnie" doing the best he could, and that his rations and surroundings were but little better than ours — a fact that we have been slow to acknowledge, but nevertheless it is true. We were totally deprived of our liberty; there was the rub.

It is related that during a troublesome period in France an old man over sixty years of age, Parisian born, who had never been outside the city in his life, became mixed up in some political trouble and was taken before the authorities who, doubting his complicity, sentenced him to remain within the city limits under police surveillance. The deprivation of his liberty was more than the old man could bear and he died in a few months.

Once a prisoner is within the stockade, parole is nearly as rare as the proverbial "hen's teeth," and after November, 1863, exchange of prisoners appeared to be forgotten, particularly as far as the Washington authorities were concerned. We will fully diagnose that monstrous policy later on in this unpolished and truthful volume.

There were instances of prisoners, both North and South, who took the oath of allegiance to the Government holding them as prisoners, for the sake of regaining their liberty; but to the everlasting honor of the men in blue and gray, these were isolated cases in comparison to the immense number who were prisoners of war and who persistently refused so to bargain away their liberty.

There were thousands of prisoners at Belle Isle, Salisbury, and Andersonville, and at Rock Island, Camp Douglas, and Elmira, who died rather than sacrifice their honor.

Dan Finch, however, regained his liberty legitimately, for we received a letter from him while at Baltimore, and another when he reached his parents' home, which was somewhere in central New York, in Cortland County, if I am not mistaken. Soon after, a comrade prisoner of his received a letter from him stating that he had rejoined his regiment. It had been recruited in Illinois, where Finch was living at the time.

I was early in life convinced of the inspired wisdom in which the "good-book" abounds, and I sincerely hope that Mark Twain was not in a jocular mood when he advised the clergyman to read the Bible, for he would find it interesting and instructive.

What a world of truth, wisdom, logic, and valuable advice there is in that biblical quotation, "A soft answer turneth away wrath, but grievous words stir up anger."

I have always, since the time when as a Sunday-school boy I committed those lines to memory, adopted the advice as a motto for future guidance. There is also a world of truth and logic — not exactly synonymous with the above, however — in Ella Wheeler Wilcox's "Laugh and the world laughs with you, weep and you weep alone."

I had a leaning toward both the scriptural injunction and that sentiment of Ella Wheeler Wilcox's, but Dan Finch was the very personification of both.

Touching my treatment on the whole, I cannot recall a solitary instance, during the fourteen months while I was a prisoner, of being insulted, browbeaten, robbed, or maltreated in any manner by a Confederate officer or soldier.

The books written by other Union soldiers who were prisoners in the South teem with accounts of the brutality, insults, and suffering heaped upon them by rebel officers and guards, seemingly for cruelty's sake. I cannot question the veracity of those Northern writers, but I can and will speak for myself, so far as I was concerned, and as to my experience and as to what came under my observation. With all respect to my late brethren-in-arms in prison life I cannot but think that to some extent they were instrumental, if they state facts, in bringing this treatment upon themselves. Did they give the "soft answer" when questioned? I do not hold that the prisoner when questioned should be obliging to the extent of giving information; but he can be courteous in his refusal to do so.

When General Hill questioned me at Liberty Mills he was very courteous, even genial. I tried to be even more polite and deferential, but he did not get a tithe out of me other than what he already knew; and that hero and gentleman — for he was both — showed neither irritation nor disappointment in his interview with me. He asked me more than a score of questions, nearly all of which I could have definitely answered to his satisfaction, but I wobbled and he knew it, and he dismissed me with a smile and said, "You are certainly a smooth-bore Yankee."

Human-nature is much the same, North and South, East and West. Civility begets civility. Josh Billings once wrote, "It is unreasonable to expect a man rising from a sudden fall on the ice to beem with cheerfulness." Upon being captured our boys could not beam with cheerfulness, it is true, and I know that many of them were curt and irritable in their intercourse with the guards.

A detachment of Union soldiers were once surrounded and captured in a piece of timber. When
they realized that it was all up with them the most
of the battalion dropped their muskets, but one of
the boys retained his until a rebel soldier was about
to reach for it, whereupon the Federal sprang
back, caught the musket near the muzzle in both
hands, and swinging it over his head smashed it
against a tree. "Now, damn you, pick up the
pieces!" he ejaculated.

"What execrable manners!" exclaimed Madame
de Stael when Napoleon bluntly and in non-tea-
table language refused to grant some political favor
for which she importuned him. "It's a pity that
one so great was so badly brought up."

The bravery and loyalty of the musket-destroy-
ing soldier was extolled in the North from "Dan to
Beersheba," and every town and hamlet between
the two Portlands was made acquainted with the
incident. If this soldier is alive to-day it is safe to
say that he hasn't got through recounting the abuse,
insults, and misery that were heaped upon him
while a prisoner in the South.

A soldier of the type of Dan Finch stripe would,
with a smile, forced though it might have been,
have quietly handed over his gun, with some pleasant remark about the fortunes of war, and made a
friend of his captor.

Upon surrendering his musket, Dan would make
a little speech, no doubt, for he was boiling over
with loquacity. It would be something like this,

"In consideration of your good fortune and valor, I have the honor to present you with this musket, no longer of any apparent use to me. Take it, dear sir, and with it my blessing." And the gloom would have been somewhat dispelled by a hearty laugh all around. I always found the rebel had a keen appreciation of a joke; he would even enjoy telling a joke on himself.

Dan Finch was every whit as good and true a soldier as the one who destroyed his musket. His comrade said he was valiant and brave and a daredevil on the fighting line, but he showed none of it at Belle Isle. There he was as non-combative and as meek as a lamb, and he was wise.

A few months after I reached Andersonville, while Captain Wirz was passing me on his horse, I inadvertently raised my hand to my cap, and he returned the salute. He continued on his way, after keenly eyeing me, without a word, but he knew me when I called on him later. The salute was the beginning of our friendship. My comrades in exile rebuked me, but my act of harmless courtesy did me no harm. But I am anticipating.

At Belle Isle I first became acquainted with a number of Southern characteristic bits of speech which were new to me. I found that the part of the day which we refer to as "afternoon," with them was "evening." It seemed that any time in the day later than 12 m. was evening. "Good evening," a rebel would say to me as early as one or two o'clock in the afternoon. With them, what we would call a "pail" in the North was a "bucket," and to carry a thing, with a Southerner was to "tote it." "Plumb" was another Southern colloquation; "I am plumb tired out." The r-slighting soft Southern drawl always had a peculiar charm for me. At Belle Isle you could hear the different sectional dialects from all parts of the country; for instance, the New Hampshire or Vermont soldier who in pronouncedly nasal tones spoke of receiving his "teown beounty," but hadn't got his "keounty beounty."

On February 18, 1864, an order was issued to about one thousand of us to be in readiness for leaving Belle Isle at 9 A. M. the following morning. Our "eleven" were among those to depart. What rejoicing! We were fully satisfied that this meant nothing short of exchange, and there was great happiness among us as we marched over the bridge on our way to the cars singing "When Johnny Comes Marching Home." We were put into cars and the train pulled out on its way to Petersburg. Ah, we were going in the wrong direction; but perhaps we would change cars there for City Point or some sea-coast town. The guards told us that they knew no more than we did as to our destination, and I don't believe they did. We reached Petersburg about noon and remained there several hours, and then moved out toward the southeast. We understood that there was a railroad running directly east to City Point, and the fact that we didn't take that road looked a little ominous, but we still thought, nevertheless, that we were about to be exchanged.

Visions of home and friends loomed up before us, but we were still going south.

Next day the train was slowly traveling along in a southerly direction. We were about a week on the journey going through North Carolina and South Carolina and into Georgia. Visions of exchange were dispelled when we left the cars and stood in line before the south gate of Andersonville Prison.

This was on the 27th day of February, 1864. It was between 10 and 11 A. M. when I was ushered in. I spent the remainder of the day exploring the camp to find a favorable place for our habitation.

The camp was situated in what had been heavy pine timber, but the trees had been cut down. There was a stream of clear water running east through the prison grounds. The stockade was built of pine logs cut twenty feet long and hewed to the thickness of one foot and set in a trench five feet deep, making a wall fifteen feet high, on top of which were sentry boxes about thirty-five feet apart. The stockade was not quite completed when we arrived, but a strong force of men was at work at it. When completed it would comprise about eleven acres. There were only about 2,000 prisoners confined there upon our arrival.

We were guarded by the Twenty-fifth Alabama Infantry, veteran troops, who knew how to treat prisoners. And I said then, and have ever since said, in speaking of our guards, the Twenty-fifth Alabama Infantry, I never met the same number of men together who came much nearer to my standard of what I call gentlemen. They were respectful, humane and soldierly.

We were organized into squads of ninety, and I soon discovered that the young rebel sergeant in charge of our squad was a fine young fellow.

The ground within the enclosure, from the brook both to the north and south, sloped upward. The entrances to the prison were through two large gates on the west side, one on each side of the creek — one the "north" and the other the "south" gate. There was a small stockade-yard on the outside around each gate, and there was a street running lengthwise through the camp from each gate.

The stream running through the ground was clear, with quite a rapid current, with a fall of about five feet to the mile, and was not the "sluggish, muddy stream, without the least perceptible water motion" that some have described it. At this time the stream furnished an ample water supply.

One writer refers to the fence as a "solid wall of hewn logs set close together twenty-five feet above the ground." The wall of logs was but fifteen feet above the ground. My occupation before I enlisted was that of surveyor, and by scientific friends and those seeking favors I was often referred to as a "civil engineer," I had an eye for measurements and topography. The wall was fifteen feet above the ground.

I have read Richardson, Kellogg, Urban, Spencer, and Grigsby on Andersonville, the most of them recently, and I was and am surprised at their free-lance recklessness of description.

Let us first discuss the topographical site of Andersonville Prison. I realize that this phase of the question has been reverted to and minutely described on an average of about once in every five or six years, since Richardson first gave his views to the public early in the autumn of 1865. Nevertheless, hackneyed and weatherbeaten though the subject is, I propose to give my version of it.

The selection of the site was an excellent one. I do not propose to dilate on the beauties of a prison. I never saw a beautiful jail yet; no more did I ever see a "beautiful coffin," as I have heard it phrased.

I wouldn't advise any one to seek a prison as a good place to spend a vacation.

Of course there were suffering, hunger, and misery among the prisoners at Andersonville, and I had my share of it there. There were also hunger, misery, and suffering at Salisbury and at Rock Island, and Elmira, the two latter places right in a "land of plenty."

The Confederate officer who selected Andersonville gave evidence of his being an engineer of no mean caliber. It was testimony that in his profession he was above mediocrity. I don't believe that in the whole State of Georgia a better choice could have been made.

The place was healthful and salubrious and the water was good. The ground within the enclosure was not as has been described by an unfriendly chronicler, seemingly with malice aforethought, as "wet, boggy, miry, and a swamp." The description does not fit.

While Spencer is mistaken, to criticise mildly, in many of his charges, his first description of Andersonville is so truthful and at variance with other Northern writers that I quote him:

"Andersonville is in the richest portion of the cotton and corn-growing region of Georgia, upon the South Western Railroad, sixty-two miles south of Macon and nine miles north of Americus, the shiretown of the county of Sumter. The population at the time of locating the prison did not exceed twenty persons. The locality is healthy, being upon an elevated ridge of light sandy soil, with rolling hills all around it. The climate is mild. The coldest weather is during December and January, when the ordinary range is about 42° Fahrenheit. By barometrical observation Andersonville is 328 feet above tide water. The wells and springs and clear streams in its neighborhood are remarkable for the coolness, pleasant taste, and crystal transparency of their contents as well as for their abundant supply."*

* Ambrose Spencer, "A Narrative of Andersonville," pp. 16, 17.

There is a dearth of "wet, boggy, miry swampiness" in that description, you notice.

Now, dear reader, mind you, the above quotation is a description relative to the prison surroundings. Here is another account by the same writer, speaking of the prison (pp. 19, 20):

"A small stream of water ran through it, about five feet wide and six inches deep, which took its rise in a swamp or morass about fifty feet farther east, and consisted of a matted, tangled growth of hay and swamp myrtle, with small tussocks of grass and logs of decaying wood. The borders of the stream were swampy and of miry character, while its course was tortuous and sluggish, and its water at no time fit for use, but as is well known in that country the prolific parent of disease and death, flowing as it did, from a reservoir steeped in decaying vegetable matter and noisome from the taste of the mould through which it was filtered. A portion of this stream, with its generating marsh, was confined within the limits of the prison bounds."

As these conflicting descriptions were written by the same author in the same chapter of the same book, the reason, the why, the reader is at liberty to determine.

The first account is that of a healthy, salubrious camp, with clear, sparkling, running water, of ex-

cellent sort, while the latter description is that of
a noisome, death-dealing place, with a sluggish
stream of water running through it, disease-gener-
ating and unfit to drink.

"During all the time at Anderson," writes
Urban, "Father Hamilton was the only clergyman
who ever entered the prison, and he would not
have been admitted but for the fact that Wirz was
himself a Roman Catholic." Father Hamilton
was a Catholic priest. A little farther on in the
same volume, and in the same breath, metaphorically speaking, Mr. Urban informs his readers that
another clergyman, "a little rebel chaplain," frequently visited the prisoners. What a careless
handling of truth!

I met and conversed with both Father Hamilton and the "little rebel chaplain," and of course
they must both have been there. Both were God-
fearing philanthropists and ministering angels that
did good, holy work.

Mr. Spencer, on page 20 of his book, states that
the site of Andersonville Prison was selected by
W. S. Winder, son of Gen. John H. Winder, of
the Confederate Army, and that after he had settled upon the place "a disinterested spectator"
urged him to choose a more healthful site, and that
young Winder replied, "That is just what I'm not
going to do. I will make a pen here for the
damned Yankees where they will rot faster than
they can be sent." Reconcile all this if you can

with his description of the prison and surroundings on pages 16 and 17 of his book.

One of these lurid writers dilates upon the fact that hundreds of secessionists living adjacent to the prison — men, women and children — would come daily to enjoy the misery of the suffering Union soldiers; that they would gather in groups, having their luncheons with them, and, sitting down on the grass outside, would gaze for hours at the Yankees.

Spencer, on page 27 of his book, in describing this, says:

"Women went there day after day; forsaking more pressing demands upon their time at home and bearing their suckling babes upon their bosoms. They might be seen squatting upon the ground and gossiping in the interval, relieving the hours with dipping snuff or nursing their offspring, while they knitted socks and gloated over the novel sight of the prospect before them."

To borrow an expression from Shakespeare, "Now mark how plain a tale will put him down."

The knitting women with suckling babes upon their breasts were squatted on the grass outside the stockade. What for? To gaze at the Yankee prisoners and gloat over them. Nothing easier. Like the gun that the owner boasted could shoot around a corner, these knitting women must have enjoyed looking from the ground on the outside over a solid palisade of logs fifteen feet high while gloating over the suffering within.

The writer must have read Carlisle's history of the French Revolution, during the time the wives and daughters of the Canaille sat around the guillotine "knitting socks" while the heads of the aristocrats were being cut off.

I say this story of the knitting women is pure fiction. It is true that men, women, and children would collect at the depot upon the arrival of trains with prisoners, out of curiosity, and would sometimes congregate at and around the entrances to the grounds. These spectators were generally silent and respectful in demeanor; but the scenes described by others of howling, cursing, and threatening ruffians and screaming, insulting and mud-throwing viragoes is but a fancy of the writer. Nothing of that sort came under my observation.

CHAPTER V

DAILY LIFE AT ANDERSONVILLE

There was a quantity of small down timber, score blocks and brush in the camp, and the boys conceived the idea of building a habitation of some sort for shelter. So one day during the visit of the young sergeant in charge of our detachment we asked him how near the stockade we would be permitted to build our quarters, and he said that as soon as the stockade was completed there would be a railing about twelve feet from the palisade, a space which prisoners would not be allowed to occupy or enter. This was known as the "dead line." He cautioned us not to get our quarters within the prescribed limit. The extreme lower part of the ground was used by the prisoners for certain purposes, and we selected a site as far as possible from that quarter. When we reached Andersonville there was ample room, and to spare, and we had no difficulty in selecting an available place. The site chosen by us was at the south end of the grounds, nearly in the center east and west, and twelve feet from the palisade.

We built the house twelve by sixteen feet, three logs high at the back and four logs on each side, with a porch or "shade" in front, ten by sixteen feet, all covered with poles and brush, ingeniously constructed to shed the rain as much as possible, and it did serve its purpose fairly well. We had to exercise some ingenuity, as our building was erected without hammer or nails. T. T. Whitcomb, being a carpenter, was the master mechanic.

We had a log about eighteen feet long and eighteen inches from the ground in front of our residence, and this we used as a bench. We were very proud of our quarters, and as the prison filled up with old and new prisoners coming in almost daily, and as the habitable territory all around us was becoming densely populated, it developed that we had about the best quarters in the prison.

Of the eleven of us Michigan boys who were together at Belle Isle, we were now but ten. Poor Reuben B. Douglas died at Augusta, while en route to Andersonville. "Reube" was a fine fellow, a good soldier, a genial comrade, and he was sadly mourned and greatly missed by us. This was our first death, and we looked upon it as a sore affliction.

A Colonel Persons of the Twenty-fifth Alabama Regiment was at this time commander at Andersonville. He was so popular and so well liked by the prisoners that even Spencer and Urban speak well of him.

During the month of March, while the Alabama regiment was in command, our sergeant would occasionally, upon our promising not to attempt to escape, take us outside the stockade into the timber. We would stroll around the woods for two or three hours, and when we returned each one of us would carry back an armful of wood. We did our own cooking. At this time our rations consisted of corn meal, beans, and an occasional ration of meat — not any way sumptuous nor too plentiful.

We enjoyed the outings greatly. At the gate, when going out, the sergeant would nearly always lay aside his arms and trust to our honor to give him no trouble and return with him, and I can truthfully state here that none of my nine comrades nor myself abused the trust.

A few weeks after reaching Andersonville I was troubled with the scurvy. My gums were sore and my teeth were becoming loose. The sergeant, upon hearing of my trouble, asked me several questions and said he would help me. Next morning he brought me two or three small Irish potatoes, which he said was the best-known remedy. I found it so. There was hardly a day while his regiment was at Andersonville that he did not bring me some little gift or other in the shape of edibles. I am sorry that I have forgotten his name, for I owe him much. I was barefooted, ragged, and in poor health; a stranger in a strange land. This young fellow was a sergeant in Company A, Twenty-fifth Alabama Infantry.

One morning late in March the sergeant told me there was an express box at the depot for me, and he told me to give him a list of my friends'

names and he would ascertain if there was anything for them. I did so, and the next day he
brought in a box for me and one that had been
sent to poor Reuben Douglas, our deceased comrade. His box was delivered to me. My box contained ham, tea, crackers, cheese, salt, soap,
quinine and a brand-new necktie of the fashion of
1862. I did so need the necktie. I hardly knew
how I had existed all winter without one. But
that box was a treat! There were two nice cakes
of castile soap. Hungry though I was, I think
that I prized the soap above all. The contents of
the two boxes were divided among the ten "Michiganders," but I kept a whole cake of soap for myself.

For the preceding three weeks we had been
cooking our rations in clouds of turpentine smoke
from the pine wood, a smoke that left us as black
as full-blooded Ethiopians, and no amount of
washing and rubbing without soap had the least
effect.

As soon as the contents of the boxes were disposed of and a safe, suitable place was selected for
the necktie I took my piece of soap and went to the
creek where we did our washing and bathing.
This place, in the daytime, was always crowded,
and it was some time before I could get to the
creek. When, armed with the soap, I could get
to the water, I began active operations. Opposite to me was a half-naked boy, blackened so with
smoke that his mother would not have known him.

"Mister," said he, "please let me just get one rub of that blessed soap." I handed it to him. Then another asked me for "just a rub," and another and another. I could not refuse, and when I finally got it back the soap was half gone. After that I adopted a new plan. It was, to use a little French, a *coup d' etat*. When the sentry over my head would call, "Post number 35. Three o'clock and all is well," I would get up, take my soap, and go to the now deserted creek, strip, which did not take long, for by this time I had but a shirt and pants, and I would wash myself from the top of my head to the soles of my feet.

We were infested with vermin to a degree that, were I to describe it adequately, my account would be received with incredulity. In the hot weather the suffering from the contact and foraging of this pest was almost unbearable.

I have compared notes with Southern soldiers who were prisoners at Rock Island and at Point Pleasant, and with Confederate Officers who were at Columbus, Ohio, and an eminent jurist of Montana, Judge N. C. McConnell, a Christian and a gentleman, whose every word I believe, an ex-prisoner of Johnson's Island, who stated that to his personal knowledge the ravages of this diminutive raider were simply horrible.

Individuals in ordinary home life can form no idea of the pest because they have never been exposed to it as we were. It seemed that this parasitic insect never knew what life was until it met the soldier, and the fastidious son of Mars feared it more than a woman fears a mouse.

In my boyhood days back in Michigan, and I do not relate this to cast any reflection upon my adopted State, we had a sort of epidemic of what was known as the seven-years-itch. We looked upon it as an excruciating affliction, but at its worst it was nothing as compared to the suffering produced by this awful parasite.

And, in summing up the evidence of Union and Confederate soldiers, all good witnesses, I decide that Andersonville is entitled to the prize. It was a very Mecca of this diminutive, horrible transmigrant.

I soon found that frequent bathing was a sort of flank movement on the insect; it was more than a surprise, it was interfering with its communications. This adhering closely to the bathing plan every morning through that terrible summer of 1864 I think was the saving of my life.

We parted with our Alabama guards early in April. It was a disappointment to us, for we had found friends among them, real friends who shared with us their scant allowance. Others who had nothing "gave all they had — a tear." The Alabamians were replaced by militia and homeguards. If I am not mistaken, about this time, Gen. John H. Winder took command of Andersonville and of other Southern prisons.

This officer was thoroughly disliked by the prisoners at Andersonville, and not without cause.

He has been severely handled by other Northern writers and I do not propose to defend him. He has long since appeared before the Great Judge of all judges. He was tyrannical, and there was no denying General Winder was a military appearing man, at that time perhaps sixty years of age. In early life he had been a military cadet, and it was said got into difficulty with the authorities at West Point and would have been expelled but for the intercession of John C. Calhoun. Of this I have no knowledge except hearsay and reports that were in circulation at Andersonville; but this I do know, he was over-exacting, cruel, and tyrannical by nature. To hold him personally responsible, however, for the scant and meager rations and lack of clothing to the prisoners I think is both unjust and unreasonable, yet the little he had to give he could have given less grudgingly. As Colonel Ingersoll in one of his lectures puts it, "If you have only a penny to contribute to the needy, hand it over like a philanthropist; and if you have but a dime to spend with a friend, spend it like a prince." General Winder had an intense hatred for Union soldiers and the Federal Government, and was thereby the wrong man to be in command of helpless prisoners.

Colonel Persons was an entirely different man. He performed his duty as commandant of the prison in a most humane manner, and the escape of prisoners was not nearly so frequent an incident as after General Winder had assumed charge.

There never was an officer in command of a prison, North or South, more humane, fair, and kindhearted, and yet unswerving and conscientious in discharging the duties of his position and in loyalty to his Government, than Colonel Persons.

Even historian Spencer, bitter as he is toward the Southern Confederacy in general and the rebel prison commanders in particular, says:*

"The commandant of the post and prison at this time was Col. A. W. Persons, formerly of Fort Valley, Georgia, who was in temporary command of the Alabama regiment, then stationed as guards. The authority of Colonel Persons was not of long duration, but during the continuance of his command no special complaints were made by the prisoners of cruel treatment. His orders were mainly directed to the safekeeping of the prisoners and the supply of their commissariat.

"He allowed the prisoners to provide themselves with bushes and poles with which they could erect arbors and shelters against the weather. He permitted squads to go out daily for the purpose of obtaining fuel, which was abundant near the prison, and it is believed that, as far as his knowledge and experience of the requirements of his position permitted, he used all

---

* "A Narrative of Andersonville," pp. 25-26.

the facilities in his power to mitigate the condition in which his prisoners were placed.

"But he did nothing more. He ought to have urged the erection of barracks, however rough, to shield his prisoners from the elements."

Early in April, after the Twenty-fifth Alabama Regiment — blessings on its memory! — departed, we began to hear of Capt. Henry Wirz, or "Cap." Wirz, as the boys called him. He had command of the prisoners, or, more properly speaking, the "interior" of the stockade, which meant the same thing.

He had been in command a week or ten days before I saw him. Captain Wirz, it appeared, did not make a good impression, possibly because he was a foreigner and spoke with an accent; at any rate, reports derogatory to him began to circulate, and the story did not spoil in the telling. What one suspected was recounted to the next as a fact. I confess that in my credulity I was as prejudiced against him as any of the prisoners. The rations were cut down and the prisoners had a grievance. In fact, they began to look upon Captain Wirz as a cause of all this trouble. I afterward ascertained that the order to shorten rations reached Andersonville before Colonel Persons had left.

About this time fuel became scarce in the prison. The felled timber, score blocks, and brush that remained on the ground after the stockade was completed had all been used. The pine stumps within the inclosure had been chopped up, and even the roots dug up and used in cooking our food. The conditions were getting desperate. We couldn't get sufficient fuel to cook the rations that were issued to us raw. Some of the prisoners who had been allowed to go outside to collect fuel, I am sorry to say, broke their temporary parole and escaped and of course this had a tendency to shut down on special privileges heretofore accorded to us. Before Colonel Persons left we had been given these privileges, and now the innocent had to suffer.

My company boys, "the Michiganders," were nearly all sick. The partially cooked food aggravated the sickness. "Our boys" and several of our nearest neighbors held a meeting to discuss ways and means, and the result was that I was selected as ambassador to Captain Wirz. I had previously met him as recorded in a former chapter of this work. Meeting him in one of his rounds of the prison I approached and saluted:

"Captain Wirz, I believe," said I. "Yes, sir." "May I speak with you?" "Certainly." "Captain, there are a number of the prisoners adjacent to my quarters, several of whom are my immediate comrades, who are sick. We have no fuel with which to cook our rations. The meal issued of late is poor in quality. I think that there is part of the cob ground with it. I am here on a begging mission to see if something can not be done to remedy matters. I trust that you will pardon my presumption." "Yes, sir; you are certainly excusable and justifiable in coming to me. I realize the situation. I am doing all I can to remedy matters and to relieve the deplorable condition, but I am hampered in many ways. We are building a bakery, working day and night to complete it. There will be a change very soon; the men will soon get bread." I heartily thanked him.

The above is not the verbatim colloquy between us, but it is the substance of our conversation.

He impressed me as an unassuming, kind-hearted man, with a somewhat sad expression of countenance.

Within a day or two after this, meal of a better quality was issued to us, and a day or two later still, we received corn-meal mush, and later, bread.

And this was the man who has been charged with deliberately putting a deadly poison into vaccine matter that was used in vaccinating the prisoners, the result of which "one hundred and twenty died by vaccine-poisoning in one week."

The interview produced in my mind a complete revolution of my opinion of the man. I had gone to him with fear and trembling, looking for the worst. I had hesitated and turned back two or three times before I could conclude to speak to him, but the remembrance of his returning my salute some days previous had encouraged me. One of my comrades, after I had started, called, and overtaking me said, "Jim, come to think about it, I don't believe I'd go. It won't do any good. He will construe it into a case of mutiny and order you under arrest. No, don't go," and this cautionary advice only added to my perplexity.

The descriptions given by others of Captain Wirz are so erroneous, misleading, and untrue that I will describe him as well as I can at this late day. He was of good height, perhaps five feet eight inches; slim in build, with a handsome face, aquiline nose, even features and a high forehead. His eyes were gray in color. At this time he wore a short, partially full beard. There was a quiet, subdued expression of sadness in his countenance, particularly in his eyes. There was nothing of that "short, thick-set Dutchman, repulsive in appearance, besotted, ignorant and cruel" we hear about, or of a countenance denoting "ferocity and brutality."

I have always marveled at the descriptions of this most unfortunate man given by those who often saw him.

In May the prisoners began to arrive in great numbers. It was excessively warm even for that latitude. The guards spoke about the weather as being more than usually hot, and the poor prisoners suffered from sickness superinduced by the extreme heat.

Through the recommendation of Wirz an addition to the hospital was built, which was in charge of Dr. Josiah H. White, who, I will say, did everything in his power and at his command to alleviate the condition of the suffering patients. Some time in April or the fore part of May, Dr. R. R. Stevenson superseded Dr. White as medical director.

Chief among the surgeons were Doctors J. H. White, W. J. W. Kerr, and R. R. Stevenson. I knew them and their surroundings sufficiently to testify that no medical men, North or South, performed their duty more laboriously or conscientiously than the above-named gentlemen. They labored night and day to alleviate the suffering among the sick prisoners, and none but themselves fully realized the difficulties under which they labored. They were in constant attendance upon the sick, ministering to them and doing all in their power to heal and cure, but they were beset with all manner of difficulties — the want of medicine, the want of proper food, bedding, clothing, shelter, and in fact everything needed to make sick men comfortable.

From my observations the charge that has been so often made that these surgeons were in league with Captain Wirz to rob, and that they wilfully neglected the sick prisoners, is false.

Yet those three surgeons were indicted with Captain Wirz in these words: "That they did combine, confederate, and conspire maliciously, traitorously and in violation of the laws of war, to impair and injure the health and to destroy the lives by subjecting to torture and great suffering,

6

by confining in unhealthy and unwholesome quarters, by exposing to the inclemency of winter and the dews and burning sun of summer, by compelling the use of impure water and by furnishing insufficient and unwholesome food to large numbers of Federal prisoners, to the end that the armies of the United States might be weakened and impaired, and the insurgents engaged in armed rebellion against the United States might be aided and comforted; and so knowing and evilly intending, did refuse and neglect to provide proper lodgings, food or nourishment for the sick, and necessary medicines and medical attendance for the restoration of their health, and did knowingly, wilfully and maliciously and in furtherance of their evil designs, permit them to languish and die for want of proper care and proper treatment;" and a whole ream more of kindred charges.

Not one of the thousands of prisoners that survived Andersonville but must have known that this was a mass of falsehood, and yet these were the charges and specifications that prevailed in that unparalleled trial in October, 1865!

Grigsby, Spencer, Kellogg, and Urban allege that the hospital was inadequate. That is true. They claim that the sick prisoners had not proper accommodations. That is true. They claim that the food was not sufficiently nourishing. That is true. And that there was not proper medicine or a sufficiency of it to be used in the care of the sick is correct. But we must remember that all the time during 1864 the Confederate Government was in an impoverished condition; the troops in the field were without proper supplies and that they were limited in the hospital supplies is undeniable. The Confederate Government itself was suffering for the want of food, clothing, and medicine.

Of course there were thousands in the hospitals at Andersonville, the suffering was awful, and there were thousands of deaths, but the surgeons in attendance were no more accountable or to blame for it than babes. Neither was Captain Wirz to blame for it. I think that he and the physicians did everything in their power with the means at their command to care for the sick and to alleviate the suffering. They did their duty like Christians and like men.

Some of the Andersonville historians have published an account of Dr. Kerr "brutally striking a sick prisoner." Permit one who is familiar with the circumstances to give the correct version.

One day in August Dr. Kerr caught a hospital attendant, a paroled prisoner, selling a blanket to a guard. Dr. Kerr investigated the matter and ascertained the fact that the Federal prisoner had stolen it from a patient. He as good as caught him in the act, and when he remonstrated with the thief the latter, being a desperate man, attacked the Doctor, and but for the surgeon's agility he would have been injured. As it was his sleeve was cut through with a knife, grazing the skin, whereupon the Doctor promptly and very properly struck the thief over the head with the butt of his revolver, knocking him down and disarming him. Simply that and nothing more, except that the thief lost his detail and the sick prisoner found his blanket.

Yes, we had all manner of men among us at Andersonville, some as thorough fiends as have lived since William Kidd died, and some so false we were compelled to thin them out by hanging six of them.

Speaking of Dr. White, the medical director at Andersonville, reminds me that one of our writers on Andersonville says that "sixty barrels of whisky were received by him in August, 1864, for medical purposes and that the whisky was drunk by the medical director and his friends."* Pretty tall drinking!

---

* "A Narrative of Andersonville," pp. 104, 105.

CHAPTER VI

"THE DEAD-LINE" AND THE DEATH OF "POLL PARROT"

I think that it was about the first of May that a lieutenant with a squad of negroes began to put up a railing fifteen feet from the stockade. If I am not mistaken the lieutenant's name was Davis. They took boards about six inches wide, such as are used in fence building, and set posts into the ground every fifteen feet and nailed the boards on top of the posts. This was known as the "dead-line." I was absent when, in the course of their building, they reached our quarters, and when I returned I found my comrades very much distressed and alarmed. They told me the lieutenant and his men were there; that the officer measured the ground from the palisade and they had found that our house was three feet within the prescribed limit of the dead-line; that it was but twelve feet from the stockade, and that the officer ordered them to move it at once. This was indeed a calamity.

We were discussing the matter when the young officer appeared on the scene. We called his attention to the crowded condition of the ground about us. It was the most desirable part of the camp and in our immediate vicinity there was not a square foot of unoccupied ground.

"I cannot help it," said he; "I am carrying out my orders, and if you cannot move the cabin you will have to take it down."

There was no use expostulating with him. He left, giving us an hour, I think it was, to move our habitation. We were speechless. He returned at the specified time, flew in a rage to find that we had done nothing, and used some very strong English.

"If you care to retain your building material," exclaimed the irate officer, "you had better get it away from here in the next twenty minutes. I will give you that time." He looked at his watch with the declaration that he would return in twenty minutes, and if the building was not moved that he would confiscate the whole thing.

Some of the boys suggested taking the house down and cutting off a few feet of the logs and rebuilding it inside of the dead-line; but this plan was not feasible and I told them that I would try to see Captain Wirz at once, and in case the Lieutenant returned before I did to explain matters to him, and try and stay his hand.

The boys were dismayed at the situation, and doubted their ability to do anything with the officer in the mean time, and doubted still more that the Captain would help us.

I made as good time as a sick man could to the south gate, and fortunately I saw Wirz just entering it. I saluted and said, "'Captain, we are in serious trouble at our quarters, and we want you to help us out. I hate to bother you but you are our only refuge now." "What is the trouble?" "Before the stockade was completed a sergeant in Colonel Person's regiment stationed here directed us while building our cabin to be sure and not build it closer to the stockade than twelve feet. We followed his instructions, and to make sure of it the end nearest to the wall is twelve feet from it. Now the lieutenant building the dead-line has ordered us to move it or take it down. The space adjacent to the cabin is so densely crowded that it is impossible to move it intact, and we cannot take it down as we do not know where to locate it." "Can you not shorten it in some way?" I explained why that could not be done. "Where are you located?" "Almost directly under sentry box number 35." "Very well, I'll go up with you and see for myself." We walked with me to our quarters, two hundred and fifty yards southeast of the gate.

When we came in sight of our house I saw that it was still there and the boys were all outside, the most of them sitting on the "piazza." They arose as we approached, and I could see surprise on their countenances. Wirz looked the situation over carefully while we were narrowly eyeing him, and I caught the faintest glimmer of a smile on his face as he said, pointing with his hand to the extreme southerly end of the cabin, "Who sleeps there?"

"That is where I sleep, Captain," said I. "Well," said he, "you must be careful and not get up inside the dead-line." Then he went on, looking at all of us, "Men, let your quarters stand, and when Lieutenant Davis returns tell him that such are my orders, and not to interfere with your cabin. He can make a short offset in his line and go by without much trouble."

We heartily thanked him, and Billy Bowles was very enthusiastic over the outcome of the affair, and yelled, "Hurrah for Captain Wirz!" and we and some of our neighbors heartily joined in the cheering.

The cabin stood where it was originally built. It was not moved or taken down. This fact will be remembered by many ex-prisoners who are now living, as this incident was often referred to and discussed at the prison. We had the distinction of occupying the only house, cabin, hut, quarters, or habitation within the dead-line at Andersonville!

There was no question about the dead-line itself. It was, during the summer of 1864 at Andersonville, a stubborn fact. The railing was a well-defined sign of demarcation. It was the visible warning of "thus far and no farther," and every prisoner within the inclosure knew it. They well knew that to get within that proscribed space meant death at the hands of the sentries, and there were prisoners killed by the guards inside the dead-line at Andersonville. This was wrong.

It was cruel. It was also cruel to shoot prisoners within the inclosures of Point Pleasant and Johnson's Island, where they were confined. In this peaceful time, to the casual observer, the shooting down of poor, often sick, helpless prisoners of war inside an inclosure must seem the very height of barbarity. Nevertheless, it was done at every prison in the North and in the South. We have been for forty years denouncing the South without discovering "the beam in our own eye." It is a clear case of those "living in glass houses." But we have been imitating Aesop's wolf at the stream. As Sherman says, "War is hell."

I have read articles written by commandants of Northern prisons setting forth the fact that the rebels killed were not fired at until the sentries had first ordered them to halt or fall back. I believe this to be the absolute truth.

On the other hand, while there were Union prisoners deliberately shot down during the daytime inside the dead-line at Andersonville, or "Camp Sumter," as the rebels called it, I believe that the sentries, before firing, ordered them back. That was my understanding of the matter, as it was also the understanding of the other prisoners. We understood that the order, "Prisoner, halt; get back beyond the line!" or a similar command must precede the act of firing.

There were well defined "neighborhoods" at Andersonville, and one day in the latter part of July a prisoner in our "neighborhood" was killed by a sentry. I am not sure whether it was the sentry at post 34 or 36; but at any rate, the rumor had it that the sentry fired without a word of warning and killed the unfortunate prisoner. The charge was contradicted by others living near the sentry box. It was also stated that the poor prisoner was partially deaf and did not hear the warning, and from his intense suffering he had become somewhat demented. At any rate, he was killed. I talked with Captain Wirz about the affair and from what he said I was satisfied that his orders to the guards were not to fire unless the prisoner failed to halt or return beyond the line. Said he, "I will investigate this matter." The sentry who had done the shooting was not seen at the post afterward.

Some of our writers boldly assert that no command to halt or warning was given before the shooting; that sentries were keenly on the alert to find a prisoner inside the line to fire on him, because for every prisoner killed within the dead-line the sentry was entitled to a thirty days' furlough. These same writers claim that prisoners with a leg or arm within the dreaded inclosure, and even the prisoner who would inadvertently place his hand on the railing, was killed. This is a monstrous charge!

One of those Andersonville writers, the loudest in maintaining that no warning was given by the sentries, rather stumbles in his statements, for he relates a case of a deaf prisoner who "did not hear the command to halt" and "was ruthlessly shot down."

The report of the "thirty days' furlough" for the sentry who shot a man within the dead-line was rife at Andersonville, but it was the easiest thing imaginable to start a rumor. No, statement, no matter how weird, wonderful, improbable, wild or incredible, once started in the prison, would fail to have its couriers, its relators, and its believers.

We had a small-pox scare among the prisoners quite early in the history of the prison. There were a few sick within the inclosure who were brought down by the terrible malady. These persons were hurriedly and promptly taken from us and isolated; a commendable act upon the part of Captain Wirz and the medical men.

There was an order for prompt and immediate vaccination, but the prisoners who could show that they had been treated shortly before were not interfered with. Others were vaccinated with fatal results in many cases. Many of those were compelled to go to the hospital, whereupon some garrulous individual started the fire that has never been quenched, viz. that there was poison in the vaccine matter. The truth is, the poison was in the impoverished blood of the patient, which could not grapple with varioloid, and not in the vaccine matter.

The so-called "dead-line" was a thing maintained in prisons, both North and South, during the Civil War. The line itself was a reality, there was no guess-work about it. To pass beyond it and to refuse or fail to halt or turn back when ordered by the sentry meant death, or at the very least a severe wound. The prisoner knew that he was taking his life in his hands when he crossed the dead-line and ignored the commands of the sentry.

I do not propose to argue as to whether it was right or wrong; that it was cruel admits of no denial, but it appears to be recognized by the rules of war.

According to the rules of war the soldier deserting "in the face of the enemy" merits death, and the soldier striking his superior officer and one who knowingly and wilfully disobeys the orders of his superior officer, upon conviction by court-martial, cannot expect less.

I have now given my opinion of the dead-line, humble and inconsequential though it may be; at all events, authorities, both North and South, considered this war measure necessary.

The guards at all the prisons were but few in comparison to the number of prisoners. It is true that the guards were armed, but they could have been overpowered with little difficulty had there not been strict discipline and certain restrictions placed upon the prisoners. At the time that there were more than 30,000 prisoners at Andersonville I do not think the guards numbered over 800.

A great deal has been said by other writers about the hundreds upon hundreds of prisoners killed within the dead-line, but I say right here that the number was few, and I deny the further assertion that some were killed who only had one foot accidentally outside the line or unintentionally laid their hands upon the railing which marked the dead-line. So far as my knowledge of Andersonville goes, the statement is untrue.

John McElroy, who wrote "A Story of Rebel Prisons," and who was a prisoner at Andersonville, and, with the exception of Mr. Spencer, the most bitter and unfair against Captain Wirz and the rebels, says (pp. 156, 157):

"The only man I ever knew to be killed by the Twenty-sixth Alabama (the regiment guarding Andersonville) was named Hubbard, from Chicago, and a member of the Thirty-eighth Illinois. He was continually hobbling about chattering in a loud, discordant voice, saying all manner of hateful and annoying things wherever he saw an opportunity. This and his beak-like nose gained for him the name of 'Poll Parrot.' His misfortune caused him to be tolerated where another man would have been suppressed. By-and-by he gave still greater cause for offense by his obsequiousness to curry favor with Wirz, who took him outside several times for purposes that were not well explained. Finally, some hours after Poll Parrot's visits outside, a rebel officer came in with a guard and proceeded with suspicious directness to a tent which was the mouth of a large tunnel that a hundred men or more had been quietly pushing forward, broke the tunnel in, and took the occupants outside for punishment. The questions that demanded immediate solution then were, 'Who is the traitor? Who informed the rebels?'

"Suspicion pointed very strongly to Poll Parrot. By the next morning the evidence collected seemed to amount to a certainty, and a crowd caught the Parrot with the intention of lynching him. He succeeded in breaking away from them, and ran under the dead-line near where I was sitting in my tent. At first it looked as if he had done this to secure the protection of the guard. The latter, a Twenty-sixth Alabamian, ordered him out. Poll Parrot arose, put his back against the dead-line, faced the guard, and said in his harsh, cackling voice, 'No, I won't go out. I have lost the confidence of my comrades and I want to die.'

"Part of the crowd were taken back by this move, and felt disposed to take it as a demonstration of the Parrot's innocence. The rest thought it was a piece of bravado because of his belief that the rebels would not injure him after he had served them. They renewed their yells, the guard ordered the Parrot out again, but the latter, tearing open his blouse, cackled out, 'No, I won't go; fire at me, guard. There's my heart; shoot me right there.'

"There was no help for it, the sentry leveled his gun and fired. The charge struck the Parrot's lower jaw and carried it completely away, leaving his tongue and the roof of his mouth exposed. As he was carried back to die he wagged his tongue vigorously in attempting to speak, but it was of no use.

"The guard set his gun down and buried his face in his hands."

The above is a garbled account. Mr. McElroy states facts as far as he goes, but he doesn't go far enough.

In the first place, the shooting of Hubbard occurred at least two months after the Alabama regiment left Andersonville — the Twenty-fifth instead of the Twenty-sixth, as McElroy puts it. It was was some time about the middle of June that this occurred. Hubbard had lost his right leg at Chickamauga and had come a prisoner to Andersonville as early as April. He was an inoffensive, garrulous creature, and on account of his almost helpless condition had received favors at the hands of Captain Wirz. This tunnel that Mr. McElroy described was in the immediate vicinity of our cabin and some of my friends were concerned in the work. It was not generally known at the time, but later on we ascertained the fact that the Confederate authorities had one of their men disguised as a prisoner among us as a night spy. We subsequently learned he was busy spying about of nights. Several tunnels were started in the prison, and it was a surprise to us how readily the guard could locate them.

Before our knowledge of this spy's presence and

work among us suspicion pointed to this prisoner or that as the informer. Hence, poor Hubbard became the victim.

My personal acquaintance with Hubbard led me to believe him innocent. I walked by the side of Hubbard on his way to the south gate, where he was followed by the mob charging him with being a traitor and declaring that if he did not get out of the stockade they would kill him. I had great sympathy with the man, doubting then, as I do now, that he had any knowledge of the location of the tunnel. When he reached the small gate in the dead line at the main entrance he pushed through, disregarding the command of the sentinel to halt, and sat down on the ground four or five feet outside of the dead-line, out of reach of the mob. Here he sat with his crutches across his lap and rocked his body back and forth, bewailing his fate, and when ordered back by the sentinel, with the threat that if he did not go he would shoot, he bared his breast and told him to shoot, that he would rather be killed by him than by his own comrades.

The sentinel called for an officer, and Captain Wirz appeared from the outside. Upon learning the cause of the disturbance Captain Wirz talked to the excited prisoners for several minutes, assuring them that Hubbard was innocent; that he had frequently taken him outside for recreation and food, and urged them to withhold their wrath and let him come back into the prison. He turned to

Hubbard and told him to go back inside, that the boys would not harm him, and then he withdrew. The guard ordered poor "Poll Parrot" out three times, and then shot him dead, the ball passing through his head and breaking his well leg.

The sentry performed this duty reluctantly. He was goaded to the act by the taunts of the prisoners seeking Hubbard's death, shouting to him, "You are a tin soldier, a wooden soldier!" and such taunts because he delayed firing. When he had at length fired the fatal shot he set down his musket and buried his face in his hands.

The clamor and violence of our prisoners, the passion of a howling mob, drove a poor, heart-broken, one-legged fellow-prisoner to his death.

Thiers, in his "History of the French Revolution," says "a mob is insane." I believe it.

After Hubbard died those who had been the loudest crying for his death were the busiest explaining why and how they knew that he was innocent.

I never could understand why Captain Wirz was condemned and executed at Washington, on November 10, 1865, unless it was for the murder of poor "Poll Parrot."

Captain Wirz had no kindergarten to deal with. The very fact that we were reluctantly compelled to put six of our own fellow-prisoners to death in order to maintain discipline shows the difficulty the commandant had to grapple with.

7

I have carefully read Spencer's account of the court martial of Wirz, and the evidence and addresses of counsel for the prosecution and defense, and there is not one word of evidence introduced touching upon the fact that we ourselves executed six of our comrades; but no one will deny that this gang, possibly with one exception, richly deserved death.

CHAPTER VII

THE STANTON POLICY

It was estimated in June that there were 20,000 prisoners at Andersonville, and through the recommendation of Captain Wirz preparations were begun to enlarge the prison, which was increased to about twenty-one acres. It was completed July 1, and was of inestimable benefit to the large number, which was daily being augmented.

July 1 was moving day for thousands of prisoners who had been cramped for sufficient room, and there was a perfect stampede for the new portion. It was found that the clay in the new ground was suitable for the making of brick or adobe by mixing it with water, and many of the prisoners availed themselves of the opportunity to go into the brickmaking business. A great many of them built the walls of their huts out of this "adobe," which hardened sufficiently in the sun for that purpose.

There were all kinds of men, "good, bad, and indifferent," among the prisoners. The general majority of them, however, were God-fearing men, who had received religious instruction during childhood. These were desirous of forming some way to hold religious meetings, but heretofore the

crowded condition of the prison had interfered
with any such plan; but after July 1 hundreds of
the prisoners held a meeting headed by one of the
number named Shepard, a chaplain of the Ninety-
seventh Ohio. At home he had been a minister.
Boston Corbett, a corporal in a New Jersey regiment, and who afterward became famous as the
"Sergeant Corbett" who shot John Wilkes Booth,
the assassin of Lincoln, assisted Elder Shepard in
this religious movement.

I well remember the text of the first sermon
preached by our good elder. It was: "But even
the very hairs of your head are numbered. Fear
not, therefore. Ye are of more value than many
sparrows."

The leaders of the "praying band," as they were
flippantly referred to by some of the irreligious
prisoners, succeeded in getting possession of a
spot of ground in the new part of the inclosure for
the purpose of holding regular religious meetings.
At these gatherings, which were well attended, the
prisoners seated themselves on the ground, and
after a sufficient number had assembled, some
would open with prayer and then Elder Shepard or
Corporal Corbett would preach a short sermon or
exhortation and close with singing and prayer.
These meetings did a world of good.

There was an insufficiency of medicine and of
nourishing food. The Federal authorities had declared medicine contraband and the whole South

was suffering for the want of quinine and other necessary drugs.

But, bad as was the physical condition of the prisoners, their mental depression was worse and more fatal. Acclimation, unsuitable diet, and despondency were the potent causes of disease and death.

The effects of salt-meats and farinaceous food without vegetables were manifest in the great prevalence of scurvy. The scorbutic condition thus induced modified the course of every disease, poisoned every wound, however slight, and was the primary cause of those obstinate and exhausting cases of dysentery which swept off thousands of our poor prisoners,

As early as July Captain Wirz, at the recommendation of the medical staff, put into operation the brewing of "corn beer," and this was given to those suffering from scurvy, and it had a most salutary effect in checking the trouble, as it acted as an antidote to the scorbutic poison. The beer was made from corn meal and also from whole corn being scalded in hot water and a mash made of it; some yeast was added to it to promote fermentation, and in a few days a sharp acid beverage was produced, very wholesome and palatable. This same corn beer was made within the stockade by the prisoners, but not to the extent that it was manufactured on the outside, nor of so good a quality.

Captain Wirz did not rest here. He lent assistance to some of the prisoners within the inclosure to make the beer. A prisoner known as "Limber Jim," afterward our chief of police, obtained a barrel or small tub and some utensils from Wirz and started quite a little distillery.

I have gone into the corn beer subject at considerable length for the reason that none of the Andersonville writers have had the fairness to mention Captain Wirz's name in connection with the subject. It wouldn't do even to hint that Wirz was instrumental in introducing a beverage that was so beneficial to the poor, sick prisoners.

But all that Wirz and his staff of medical men could do failed to stop the ravages of disease and death.

The report was brought to us by the incoming prisoners that the authorities had about shut down on exchanging prisoners. "Who enter here leave hope behind" was now fully exemplified. As yet it was only a surmise, but a few weeks later, or about the first of August, we heard the cold-blooded and atrocious ukase from Edward M. Stanton, that exchange of prisoners was at an end. "We will not exchange able-bodied men for skeletons," and "We do not propose to reinforce the rebel army by exchanging prisoners."

Ah, now it was a certainty. We realized that we were forsaken by our Government. The war office at Washington preferred to let us die rather than exchange us!

The refusal upon the part of our Government

to exchange prisoners was now an assured fact. The sick lost hope and died. Those in better condition physically became disheartened and sick. It is no wonder that during August nearly 3,000 prisoners died at Andersonville.

The natural local peculiarities at Andersonville were not, as I have explained, of themselves of a character to induce any excessive mortality. The spot was selected mainly with a view to its salubrity, and this is abundantly proved by the fact that very few of our men who were out on parole died. There were about one hundred on parole during June, July and August, doing all kinds of work.

Albert D. Richardson, in his "Field, Dungeon, and Escape," written as early as 1865, says (p. 417):

"The Government held a large excess of prisoners, and the rebels were anxious to exchange man for man; but our authorities acted upon the cold-blooded theory of the Secretary of War, that we could not afford to give well-fed, rugged men for invalids and skeletons."

Again, on page 457:

"Those 5,000 loyal graves at Salisbury will ever remain fitting monuments of rebel cruelty and the atrocious inhumanity of Edwin M. Stanton, who steadfastly refused to exchange prisoners."

Melvin Grigsby, a prisoner at Andersonville, in his history of that prison, says (p. 138):

"I do not know who was responsible for that fearful blunder, but a blunder it was [the refusal to exchange prisoners]. The prison authorities [at Andersonville] permitted the prisoners to send to Washington three of their number, chosen for that purpose, who took with them a petition to the President asking them that an immediate exchange be agreed to on the terms proposed by the rebels, and setting out fully and plainly the suffering that was being endured and the loss of life daily occurring. This petition was signed by thousands of prisoners, and is probably now on file among the records of the War Department. There are many thousand gravestones at Andersonville which would not be there, and many thousand widows and orphans caused by the mistaken zeal and cold-blooded principles of those in authority at that time.

"When it was all over and thousands of the poor, emaciated creatures that survived were sent home, and scattered through the land, and the truth became known, and *Harper's Weekly* and other illustrated papers sent out pictures of the starved heroes, then a storm of indignation arose which threatened to burst over the heads of the misguided statesmen who had refused to exchange. Then something must be done, Andersonville must be avenged; the storm must be averted, and something was done; Andersonville was avenged, Wirz was hung."

This is exactly as it reads in Mr. Grigsby's book. It appears that he started out to be honest and tell the truth, but toward the end evidently weakened, or the thought occurred to him that in the one hundred and thirty-seven pages of his work he had denounced Captain Wirz unstintedly, placing the whole blame of Andersonville solely and simply upon that unfortunate man.

John W. Urban, another Andersonville prisoner, who wrote "Battlefield and Prison Pen," says (p. 381):

"We could not help contrasting this with our miserable condition; and is it strange that we sometimes felt embittered against the Government for not making a greater effort to release us? But as true as needle to the north pole, so were the most of the Union soldiers confined in Southern prisons to the Government they had sworn to defend. They might feel themselves slighted, neglected, or even deserted by the Government and among themselves be tempted to say some bitter things; but a word or insinuation to that effect from their enemies would excite their ire and indignation to the utmost and they were always ready to defend the Government from the charge that it was not doing all it could to release them. It was, however, a sad fact that hundreds died with the fear

haunting them that it was so. Men who had
cheerfully faced death on many a battlefield, lay
down and died broken-hearted as the terrible suspicion forced itself into their minds that the Government they loved so well, and fought so hard to
save, was indifferent to their sad fate."

Exchange was at an end. Consternation
reigned. Terror, amazement and despair were
plainly depicted upon the countenances of the poor,
forsaken prisoners.

Many of the prisoners, being but human, raised
their clenched, trembling hands toward heaven and
with fearful oaths cursed the authorities at Washington, the Government, the North and the South,
and the day they were born.

Oh, what a hatred was then engendered for our
Secretary of War! Ex-soldiers, North and South,
and non-combatants and civilians may talk and
think as they please, and notwithstanding all that
has been said pro and con, Edwin M. Stanton at
that time was classed in their hatred with Winder,
Wirz, Davis, and Barrett. It is true that after we
were finally released we tried to forget, and for
policy sake, I believe, either kept silent or perhaps
joined in the clamor against Wirz.

Then there was quibbling and subterfuge.
"The South refused to exchange a negro prisoner
for a rebel prisoner"; "The rebels would not exchange on an equitable basis as to relative rank of
officers"; "The rebel Government resorted to

frivolous pretexts to delay exchange, as death was doing its work at Andersonville, Salisbury, and other prisons." The Confederacy would not concede this nor agree to that, and other similar theories were given. There was charge and refutation; words, words, words.

Aesop relates that a wolf and a lamb once simultaneously went to a stream to drink, whereupon the wolf accused the lamb of roiling the water to prevent him from drinking. "How can that be," said the lamb, "when you are above me and the water flows from you to me?" "Oh, that's a subterfuge," replied the wolf, "and at any rate your tribe has always injured the poor wolves, never allowing them to live in peace, and I shall now punish you for it." So he killed the lamb and felt appeased. Allowing that it was true that the Confederate authorities refused to exchange negro soldiers for rebel soldiers, did it better the condition of the poor negro held as a prisoner to have no exchange of white Union soldiers?

Grigsby, on page 137 of his Andersonville story, says:

"As a matter of pure principle this was probably correct, but as a matter of public policy and of justice and mercy to the white soldier, who had enlisted before there were any freed negroes, it was all wrong. If there had been any considerable number of negro soldiers in the prisons suffering with the others, then there

would have been a vital principle of justice as well
as honor at stake, and the white prisoners themselves would have been the last men in the world
to have sacrificed that principle in order to secure
their own liberty and lives. There was not a
negro soldier in Andersonville or in any other
prison for a considerable time. When they were
captured they were either sent back to their old
masters or put to work on rebel fortifications, and
they were not starved and did not suffer. Their
condition as prisoners was little worse than it had
always been before the war. Stanton and others
who insisted on that point, might as well have insisted that every black in the South, whose liberty
had been granted him by the Emancipation Proclamation, and who was detained by his old master,
should be a subject of exchange."

When the Andersonville emissaries returned
from Washington there was not one word about
the exchange of the negro soldiers being in the way
of our release. It was not then thought of. I
know that for the past forty-two years that matter
has been published broadcast in the North as a
reason why we were not exchanged.

Grigsby is right in this. The Washington authorities had concluded to stop the exchange before there were any negro prisoners.

General Grant in his "Memoirs" bluntly but
honestly gives the reason for not exchanging prisoners. It seems that it was decided at Washington

that exchange meant the reinforcemen: of the rebel army, and he goes on to explain that the exchanged rebel soldier behind barricades and fortifications fighting on the defensive was equivalent to three Union soldiers attacking him.

This was the Stanton policy, and if this atrocious and inhuman doctrine is anyway meritorious, the "War Secretary" is entitled to the credit.

CHAPTER VIII

EXECUTION OF THE RAIDERS

Early in May it developed that the prison camp was infested with an organized band of thieves and cutthroats who committed their depredations upon sick and helpless prisoners. At first they confined their operations to the darkness of night, but, becoming emboldened, stronger in number and organization, they got so they did not hesitate to attack their fellow-prisoners in the daytime. The leaders of this band of "raiders," as we called them, were thieves, bounty-jumpers, "wharf-rats," and graduates generally from the schools of corruption in large cities.

This band was daily being augmented as the number of prisoners increased, and by the first of June it seemed from their activity and their audacity that more than half the able-bodied prisoners belonged to the dreaded gang, and as yet there was no organization to oppose them.

Robberies became common even in the daytime. Men were robbed of everything of value — money, watches, rings, blankets, clothing, and even of their scanty rations. The gang had the camp intimidated, and seemed to have such absolute control that the report went about the camp that Wirz was in league with them. This I never for a moment believed. A reign of terror existed. We were a large and growing community without a government.

By the earnest request of the leading prisoners in my neighborhood, on June 7 I sought and obtained an interview with Wirz. I explained the situation briefly and asked his advice and assistance. After considering a moment, he said, "I understand the condition and have been wondering what the outcome would be. I can see only one way now. If you men can organize a sufficient force to arrest those scoundrels, and bring them to the gates, letting me know when you begin operations, and when you are ready to turn them over, I will arrange to have guards to take charge of them. Then you can organize a court of some kind, get your witnesses and men to take charge of the prosecution and defense, and I will let you prisoners take charge of the whole matter. You can then come outside and try them. Now, if you prisoners conclude to undertake this, and you certainly ought to do something, keep me apprised of your progress and I will be only too glad to assist you as far as in my power. I will at once present the matter to General Winder."

As to whether or not I was the first prisoner to approach Captain Wirz relative to this matter, I do not know, but he acted as if the subject had not been broached to him before.

It was evident that Wirz gave this his prompt attention, by the following general order, which is a matter of record and speaks for itself:

"Camp Sumter, Andersonville, Ga.,

"June 30, 1864.

"General Orders No. 57.

"A gang of evil-disposed persons among the prisoners of war at this post having banded themselves together for the purpose of assaulting, murdering, and robbing their fellow-prisoners, and having already committed all of these deeds, it becomes necessary to adopt measures to protect the lives and property of the prisoners against the acts of these men, and in order that this may be accomplished, the well-disposed prisoners may, and they are hereby authorized to, establish a court among themselves for the trial and punishment of such offenders.

"On such trials the charges will be distinctly made with specifications setting forth time and place, a copy of which will be furnished the accused.

"The whole proceeding will be kept in writing, all the testimony will be fairly written out as nearly in the words of the witnesses as possible.

"The proceedings, findings, and sentence in each case will be sent to the commanding officer for record, and if found in order and proper, the sentence will be ordered for execution.

"By order of Brig. Gen. John H. Winder.

"W. A. WINDER,
"Asst. Adjutant General,"

Not a solitary writer of the many stories of Andersonville that I have read since the war has been disposed to do justice to Captain Wirz, and they have done him a great injustice in this matter. So far as I know, the idea that brought about the overthrow of the murderous raiders came from Wirz himself; and it is certain that the efforts of "Limber Jim" (James Laughlin), Key, Corrigan, Larkin, Johnson, and others, of the "law and order" organization, and of the police force, all of whom deserve great credit in arresting the "raiders," would have been fruitless but for the co-operation of Wirz.

From this time on the great question was how to meet and break up the thieving organization, but no real action was taken until the last of June. It is my recollection that the police organization was perfected on July 1. The "raiders" were not idle. They knew of the character and scope of our work as soon as we began. On July 1 Captain Wirz was notified the work of arresting suspects would begin the following day, July 2.

During three days, July 2, 3 and 4, we arrested one hundred and seventy-five men and turned them over to the guards at the south gate. There were many witnesses, and the trial lasted six days, and resulted in the conviction of six on the charge of murder in the first degree. These men were sentenced to be hanged July 11. Their names were as follows: Charles Curtis, Company A, Fifth

8

Rhode Island Infantry; Pat Delaney, Company E, Eighty-third Pennsylvania Volunteers; F. Sullivan, Seventy-second New York Volunteers; A. Muer, of the United States Navy; J. Sarsfield, One Hundred and Forty-fourth New York Volunteers, and Wm. Collins, Company D, Eighty-eighth Pennsylvania Infantry. Collins was known in the camp as "Mosby," having received the sobriquet from his daring and rushing proclivities. Had he exhibited the same spirit of dare-deviltry on the field of battle that he did in waylaying his fellow-prisoners it might have redounded to his military distinction.

Twenty-five of the convicted men were sentenced to wear ball and chain during their imprisonment.

One of the most startling developments to me in this trial was the conviction of Pat Delaney of murder. We had been neighbors in our prison life for many months, both at Belle Isle and at Andersonville. He was sent from Belle Isle with the same detachment that my comrades were. He was always ready to help others and appeared to take great pleasure in doing some kind act for my comrades and myself. He appeared always to have money and plenty to eat, and he was extremely generous with both. I was under many obligations to him, and I always regarded him as a brave, generous Irishman. A chapter could be written on the generous qualities of this unfortunate man. I sought to save him, but was confronted with overwhelming testimony of his guilt. To me it looked like a case of "poor dog Tray." It was agreed upon beforehand among the regulators that the guilty would have to take their medicine.

The court conducting the trial was regularly organized and officered, and the proceedings were regularly recorded, with the intention of making a full report later to the Government.

On the morning of the 11th a team loaded with materials for the gallows was sent in by Wirz, and our men, who were carpenters, erected the gallows in the street seventy-five yards east from the dead-line at the south gate.

A solid mass of prisoners gathered about the place, and at two o'clock Wirz came in riding his gray horse, at the head of the six doomed men, who were heavily guarded. The condemned men, tied together, walked in double file, Delaney and Curtis in advance. At the foot of the platform the Captain gave the command "halt," and turning toward us he said, "Here, men, I return these prisoners to you in as good condition as I received them. I have carried out my part of the agreement, and now whatever you may do with these men I must remind you that the Confederate Government is in no way responsible. You will do with them as you please, and may God have mercy on you and them."

With all McElroy's prejudice against Wirz he cannot strip this speech of its evident fairness. His version of the incident, given in his story of

Andersonville, is different, I know, but I was standing at this time within a few feet of the gallows.

After turning the culprits over to the police, Wirz and his guard withdrew, and I heard Curtis say, "Delaney, what do you propose to do about this? As for me, I am going to make a break." At this he slipped the cord from his wrist, and broke through the dense crowd of prisoners like a mad bull. His attempted escape created great excitement, and a shell or two went singing over the prison, I presume to remind us that our guards were ready for business and would allow no stampede toward the gate. Laughlin (Limber Jim), the sheriff or marshal of the day, despatched several of the police after Curtis, and the hangman led the other five up the steps onto the platform. They were placed on the trap under the cross-bar, from which were dangling six nooses. The condemned men were placed in position and each noose adjusted. Curtis was soon brought back and placed in position, and all was ready; but there was some delay, as each one of the condemned had some message to send to wife, mother, or friend. Some of them did not expect to die. I do not think that Delaney thought that the "regulators" would take extreme measures, for he smiled as the noose was placed around his neck. Laughlin ordered the caps (meal bags) to be drawn over their heads. The trap was sprung and five of them swung into eternity. The rope around Collins's neck broke and he fell to the ground, apparently unhurt. He rose to his feet and begged piteously for his life, but Laughlin laid his hand on his shoulder and said, "Collins, words are useless now. You are condemned to die and die you must." Then Collins regained his composure, mounted the steps with firmness, took his place beside the quivering, dangling bodies, and died without a word.

After Delaney was sentenced I had a talk with him. Said he, "Jim, I am innocent. I'll admit that I associated with the marauders; that I received money from them because I was hungry and starving. You know I had money, but I never assaulted a man nor stole a dollar; but here I am about to die. Ah, that is what comes of keeping bad company."

We sent for Father Hamilton, and that evening received extreme unction at the hands of the priest.

It was reported, but I did not know of it personally, that Father Hamilton begged for the life of Delaney.

Father Hamilton, a Southerner, was greatly beloved by the prisoners. He was kind to all of us, Catholic and Protestant alike. When we would ask him if there was any news of exchanging prisoners he would say, "Poor men, I have given my word not to communicate any information," and he would sadly shake his head and turn away.

Those marauders had even murdered fellow-prisoners in quest of booty. This was proved beyond doubt at the trial by good and reliable eye-

witnesses. More than one man lost his life by trying to defend himself and protect his property.
The witnesses had by threats of intimidation kept
silent, and moreover they "had troubles of their
own" to occupy their minds.

During the "reign of terror" the gang was so
powerful in numbers and strength of organization
that it controlled things and operated with a high
hand. It was a terrible state of affairs.

One morning shortly after daylight, while on
my way to the creek to wash, I came across a
prisoner, not more than three hundred feet from
our quarters, lying on his back dead. He had his
throat cut, evidently with a razor, as that was the
weapon usually used by the raiders.

But the terrible uncontrolled dominion of the
thug and murderer was at an end. We could
breathe easier, and within the lines could go and
come as we pleased day or night. Prior to the organization of the regulators we were constantly on
the lookout, and dared not venture from our
quarters after dark; for after dark the terrible
marauder had full swing.

Those who were acquitted by the court were yet
suspected guilty by the body of prisoners, and when
they were turned back into the prison they were
obliged to run the gauntlet between two lines of
their fellow-prisoners, who showered upon them so
many blows that three died from the injuries thus
received. I took no hand in this business; it
seemed to me the height of brutality. I had no

doubt at the time that some of those punished were innocent, but, however cruel, the great majority of them richly deserved what they got. "Limber Jim" (or Laughlin) took a prominent part in punishing the offenders. His brother had been robbed and killed by the raiders.

The men that were tried and punished had hundreds of friends and sympathizers among the prisoners, and July 11, 12 and 13 things looked ominous in the stockade. Threats were openly made and prisoners were massing toward opposite sides.

It was thought best among the regulators to ask Captain Wirz to parole Sergeant Key, Corrigan, "Limber Jim," and the hangmen who officiated at the execution, as a precautionary measure. This was done. Had they remained among us they would doubtless have been killed.

On the morning of July 14 the dead body of a prisoner named Heffron was found near the south gate. He was a prominent witness against the raiders, and one who had testified in the daytime. Night sessions of the trial had been held and it was a favorite time for witnesses for the prosecution to put in an appearance.

For a few days the situation looked gloomy indeed. The reign of terror threatened to grow even more frightful.

During the summer months at Andersonville there was a feeling between the "Eastern" and "Western" soldiers which in some instances amounted almost to hatred. Key, Corrigan,

Laughlin — "Limber Jim," and Larkin were from the West.

The raiders were now without a leader, and the hanging of six of their prominent members cowed them almost into submission; but had there been one of them possessed with a daring and audacity of Curtis or Collins on July 12 or 13 there would have been a battle in the prison in which no doubt many men would have been killed and wounded. It would have been a battle which the guards would have been powerless to suppress.

Meanwhile we were not idle, but kept up and added to our organization. In this we had the advantage of the raiders and their friends, for on the 12th and 13th they contented themselves with uttering threats and assaulting some of the regulators.

After Key left, Sergeant A. R. Hill, of the One Hundredth Ohio, was elected as our chief. He was a large, strong, and powerful man, twenty-eight or thirty years of age, and came into prominence at Belle Isle by "licking" Jack Oliver, the conceded champion among us.

Hill appointed several hundred policemen, who had secret passwords, and signal whistles to summon help. For the first few days of the Hill administration there was much disturbance and several fights, but the victory was on the side of the regulators, and in a few days quiet and order reigned.

The marauders were subdued, a number were punished, and "raiding" was at an end.

After Wirz, those entitled particularly to the credit of bringing about order and tranquilizing affairs were Sergeant Key, of an Illinois regiment; Laughlin, Larkin, Corrigan, Johnson, and others whose names I do not recall.

My reason for going into this matter to considerable length is that the other writers have treated the affair so meagerly and have withheld the credit due to Wirz.

I have at hand five histories of Andersonville. Some of the writers dismiss the subject with a paragraph. None, except McElroy, gives the names of the men hanged. None, except Kellogg and Urban, gives any credit to Wirz, if credit it can be called. Both state the same thing, and I quote from Urban's "Battlefield and Prison Pen (pp. 326, 327):

"Robert H. Kellogg, sergeant-major of the Sixteenth Connecticut Volunteers, who was in Andersonville at the time, and who is the author of an interesting work called 'Life and Death in Rebel Prisons,' writes of that affair in the following words [speaking of prisoners daily coming in plentifully supplied with money, jewelry, etc.]: 'These newcomers afforded the raiders, or camp robbers, fresh opportunities to continue their work. They seized upon one of these and it soon proved to be a robbery in earnest. After severely beating and cutting his head they took his watch and $175 in money. He entered a complaint to Captain Wirz, and the whole camp being completely aroused, collected around with clubs and began to arrest the gang as fast as possible.' "

I refrain from further quotation, except to prove "out of their own mouths" that their histories are misleading.

Urban says again (pp. 330, 331):

"Hid in the ground where the villains stayed were found watches, money, and different kinds of weapons; also the body of a man the miscreants had put out of the way."

That statement is all right, but the following statement is all wrong (p. 331):

"The valuables were taken possession of by the rebels, who no doubt rejoiced at the proceedings, as it not only enriched themselves but also weakened their enemies."

Every article, so far as I know, that was identified by a prisoner at the trial, was turned over to the owner.

Certain authors like Richardson and Kellogg allege that a most scrutinizing and careful search was made at all the rebel prisons, and that every article, valuable or otherwise, was taken from pris-

oners and never returned; that it was robbery on
the part of rebel officers and guards.

Now for a little circumstantial or presumptive
evidence to the contrary.

The marauders — our fellow-prisoners — at Andersonville robbed their fellow-prisoners of thousands of dollars, and also more than a score of
watches, besides jewelry of various kinds and descriptions.

How about, "After it was known that there
were thieves operating, men took off their watch-
chains and watch-cords on account of the industry
of the pick-pockets."

Were the rebel officers and guards unable to see
watch-chains and watch-cords?

Let us hear the evidence of Mr. Ambrose Spencer in his book, "A Narrative of Andersonville"
(p. 72):

"As each train arrived squads of ten men were
taken into a detached building nearby, where
Wirz, R. B. Winder, and W. S. Winder were assembled. There each man was searched by Duncan and Humes, was stripped to his shirt, if he
possessed one, his shoes were closely scrutinized
and the soles examined, and the shoes themselves
appropriated if they were found worthy; the
linings of the waistbands were inspected; of course
the pockets of the pantaloons were turned inside
out and their contents appropriated. The pro-
ceeds derived from this search were turned over to

Wirz for temporary deposit, afterward to be divided fairly.

"The squads were then turned over to the sergeants of the guard, and such miscellaneous articles as their superiors did not require, or did not desire to take, were appropriated. Thence they were passed to the outside guard to be marshaled into procession for the prison. If these last harpies found anything upon the persons of the prisoners worthy of their regard, it was incontinently taken, and by the time the poor wretches formed into column the regiment that Falstaff once raised would have shown well in comparison with these.

"When they at last reached the stockade and were turned into the gates, the remnants that were left to them by the rapacious crew through whose hands they had passed were not sufficient to cover their nakedness. But there was slight comfort left the poor wretches in the reflection that they were no worse off than the 20,000 who had preceded them into this Gehenna of earthly misery, and none of these could boast themselves of being possessed of more than themselves. The picture is but faintly drawn, as the author most willingly confesses that —"

But enough of this without wishing to hear Mr. Spencer's confession.

The above-named authors, after describing how everything was taken from the prisoners, go on to state that rebel sutlers enriched themselves by charging exorbitant prices for food, clothing, blankets, tobacco, liquors, and other articles sold to the prisoners!

How about the thousands of dollars, the watches and jewelry stolen by the marauders from the prisoners, and the prisoner who had his watch and $175 in greenbacks taken, if they had been despoiled of everything they had before entering the prison?

The Andersonville histories here mentioned are in every library of note north of the Ohio River, and the skeptic can investigate for himself as to the truth or falsity of the above statements.

CHAPTER IX

THE MASS MEETING OF JULY TWENTIETH

During the month of July many thousands of new prisoners were added to our crowded camp, and the hot weather and unsanitary condition of things, added to the quality and scantiness of the rations, made our situation deplorable. During this time one of our little company, John Holcomb, died in our quarters. Soon after, or early in August, Swain, Whitworth, Monroe, and Dalzell were removed to the hospital, where they died. Sergeant Whitcomb, of Company L, was out on parole working at his trade, and on August 11 there was none left in prison of our original eleven but Billy Bowles and myself as occupants of our famous quarters.

Before Swain, Monroe, Dalzell and Whitworth were taken to the hospital I met Wirz while on one of his inside visits. He stopped his horse, and I explained to him briefly the situation and the condition of my comrades. Said I, "If something is not done for them at once, in a few days death will be the result"; and this was the substance of his reply, "I am doing all I can, I am hampered and pressed for rations. I am even exceeding my authority in issuing supplies. I am blamed by the prisoners for all of this suffering. They do not or will not realize that I am a subordinate, governed by orders of my commanding officer. Why, sir, my own men are on short rations. The best I can do is to see that your sick comrades are removed to the hospital. God help you. I cannot," and his eyes were filled with tears.

I was crying myself. The animated earnestness of his manner, the tears in his eyes, showed me how deeply he felt. I did not see him again until after he had returned from his sick-leave. He was pale and emaciated that day. His wounded arm was troubling him. I noticed this and mentioned it, but he said nothing about the fact that gangrene had set in.

His statements and demeanor made a deep impression on me. Here, thought I, is a man, "a creature of circumstances," obliged to endure the odium resulting from the sins of others.

It had become evident beyond any doubt that our Government had decided it to be a fit and necessary "war measure for repressing the rebellion" that we should be sacrificed. As this became more apparent it was so understood. The Government had passed that verdict upon us. We know it now, and it was pathetic to note the effect it had upon different dispositions, some praying, some cursing, some gambling, and others, dying with curses on their lips against the Government.

A mass meeting was called for July 20. I was unable to attend on account of sickness, but Billy Bowles, the only one left, beside myself, of our original number, attended, and brought back a set of resolutions as follows:

"*Preamble:* Apparently one of the sad effects of the progress of this terrible war has been to deaden our sympathies and make us more selfish than we were when the tocsin of battle strife first sounded in the land. Perhaps this state of public feeling was to have been anticipated. The frequency of which you hear of captures in battles, and the accounts which you have seen of their treatment, has robbed the spectacle of its novelty and, by law of nature, has taken off the edge of sensibilities, and made them less the object of interest. No one can know the horrors of imprisonment in crowded quarters but him who has endured it. But hunger, nakedness, squalor and disease are as nothing compared with the heartsickness which wears prisoners down, most of them young men, whose terms of enlistments have expired, and many of them with nothing to attach them to the cause in which they suffer but principle and love of country and of friends. Does the misfortune of being taken prisoner make us less the object of interest to our Government? If such you plead, plead it no longer. These are no common men and it is no common merit that they call upon you to aid in their release from captivity.

"There are confined in this prison from 25,000 to 30,000 men, with daily accessions of hundreds, and that the mortality among them, generated by various causes, such as change of climate, dirt, and want of proper exercise is becoming truly frightful to contemplate, and is rapidly increasing in virulence, decimating our ranks by hundreds weekly.

"In view of the foregoing facts we, your petitioners, most earnestly yet respectfully pray that some action be immediately taken to effect our speedy release, either on parole or by exchange. *The dictates of both humanity and justice alike demanding it on the part of our Government!*

"We shall look forward with a hopeful confidence that something be done speedily in this matter, believing that a proper statement of the facts is all that is necessary to secure a redress of the grievance complained of."

The above was signed by more than one hundred sergeants, prisoners, who had charge of detachments of their fellow-prisoners, the men authorizing the sergeants to sign it.

The committee selected to go to Washington to intercede for exchange were: Edward Bates, Company K, Forty-second N. Y.; H. C. Higgenson, Company K, Nineteenth Illinois; Prescott Tracey, Company G, Eighty-second N. Y.; and Sylvester Noirot, Company B, Fifth N. J. They were paroled for this purpose. It was my understanding that three of them returned to Andersonville and reported the failure of their mission.

9

In regard to those resolutions, Mr. McElroy says:

"I do not think it possible for a mass meeting of prisoners to be held without my knowing it, and its essential features. Still less was it possible for a mass meeting to have been held which would have adopted such resolutions."

Regarding Mr. McElroy's declaration that in his opinion no such meeting was held and that no such resolutions were adopted, I will simply say that he is mistaken. I'll put it no stronger.

That mass meeting was held and those resolutions were adopted. After the meeting broke up Sergeant Bowles returned to our quarters with a copy of the resolutions, and by the side of my bed, upon which I lay sick, we discussed it far into the morning. I am just as positive of the mass meeting and resolutions adopted as if I attended the meeting myself.

From what Bowles said and from what others told me the next day and for a few days following, for the subject was widely and thoroughly discussed at the time, I was and am cognizant of the living fact that our Government in general and Secretary of War Stanton in particular were censured and roundly condemned at that meeting; and that in those speeches Stanton was painted as black as McElroy has painted Wirz. One poor prisoner raised his arm during the meeting and shouted, "I hold Secretary Stanton personally responsible for my misery!"

As to Mr. McElroy's statement that the origin of those resolutions "was of a rebel source," he is mistaken.

As to the mass meeting of Union prisoners at Savannah held later, and the resolutions adopted there, to which Mr. McElroy refers, that was altogether another matter. The resolutions adopted at Andersonville were not the same. I suppose that many of those who attended the meeting at Andersonville and had a hand in drafting the resolutions, afterward participated in and gave voice to the same sentiments at Savannah, and it is more than probable they had a hand in framing the set of resolutions.

The resolutions at Andersonville were discussed and toned down before their adoption, and the bitterness was eliminated, and they were diplomatically tempered before transmission.

To say that there was no such meeting, and no such resolutions were adopted is untrue. One might as well say there was no Andersonville.

I shall discuss this incident no further but leave it to the living Andersonville prisoners to decide whether Mr. McElroy is right or whether I am

During the latter part of July Captain Wirz was taken sick. He had gangrene in an old wound received at the battle of Seven Pines, and a wound that had never healed, and about August the first he left Andersonville on a sick-leave. He had previously obtained a furlough, but remained at his post as long as he was able. While absent, reports reached Andersonville that he was dying, and it was thought he would never return to duty at Andersonville.

It might not be out of place to state here that there was "credible" testimony adduced at his trial that he killed a prisoner on the 4th of August, 1864, "whose name was unknown," and that "on or about Auguslt 20, 1864, he murdered another unknown prisoner," and that also, "on or about August 30, A. D. 1864, he deliberately killed another prisoner" whose name was unknown.

During the month that Captain Wirz was away on sick leave Lieutenant Davis was in command.

My first meeting with Wirz after his return was about September 2. He was looking poorly and was not well.

He generally rode through the prison in the morning, and often during the afternoon or evening "Little Red Cap," his orderly, mounted on Captain Wirz's mare, would visit us. This little fellow was a drummer-boy about fourteen years old, and belonged, I think, to an Ohio regiment. He was captured, and entered the prison either late in February or early in March. I know that I saw him there soon after I arrived. His name was Powell. He was a handsome, smiling-faced little fellow, wearing a red cap set jauntily on the side of his head; hence the name "Little Red Cap."

As soon as Wirz took command he paroled all the drummer boys, about, I should think, fifty in number, and he took young Powell to his headquarters and detailed him as his orderly. The commandant was very good to "Little Red Cap" and allowed him great liberties.

Some of the men, thinking that "Little Red Cap" was not a sufficiently dignified title, referred to him as "Wirz's aide-de-camp." He was a fine little fellow, and a general favorite with the prisoners and the guard.

Little Red Cap was the bearer of the order issued by General Winder approving of the sentence of the six murderers whom we executed.

It was a well-known fact at Andersonville that Captain Wirz paroled the drummers that they might escape the rigors and hardships of prison life.

Of the seven Andersonville histories that I have read in years past and have carefully and patiently perused just recently, not one word could I find referring to the parole of the drummer-boys at Andersonville.

Captain Wirz never wore a sword or saber among us to my knowledge, and one day while speaking to him I said, "Captain, I have always noticed that you never wear a sword in the prison." "The poor fellows have other reminders of the war," he replied, "without my parading with sash and sword."

"Did you get your box?" was his inquiry one morning soon after his return. "Yes, sir." "You got one before, didn't you?" "Yes, sir; I received two before." It was the third box counting the one belonging to our dead comrade, Reuben Douglas, and it contained articles greatly needed that kind friends had sent from Michigan. What a treat those boxes, with their valuable contents, were to us!

One of those boxes was sent by an old boyhood friend, Hon. E. L. Briggs, of Grand Rapids, Michigan. After I was discharged I visited him and squared accounts as far as I could, but it was a debt that could never be paid. He died about two years ago and I lost one of my best old-time friends.

So much has been written about the Confederate authorities in general, and Captain Wirz in particular, confiscating clothing, medicine, and edibles sent from the North to Union prisoners that I am constrained to state my experience regarding it. As far as my knowledge went, and from observation, and as far as I was personally concerned, I can refute those charges.

As fully as I could learn after regaining my liberty and going home these two boxes of articles were the only ones sent me while a prisoner, and I received them intact. And, moreover, I knew many other boxes containing necessary articles being received by my comrades at Andersonville. I don't believe that the Confederate authorities ever confiscated property sent to Union prisoners.

That the guards at Andersonville during the summer of 1864 were on short rations and that the authorities were unable to supply the prisoners with medicine and adequate food and clothing is a well-known fact.

In corroboration of this I will quote from a letter written by General Sherman, dated September 22, 1864, to James E. Yeatman, chairman of the Sanitary Commission, at St. Louis, Missouri:

"These Confederates are as proud as the Devil, and hate to confess poverty, but I know they are really unable to supply socks, drawers, undershirts, scissors, combs, soap, etc., which our men in prison need more than anything else to preserve cleanliness and health."

Now let us look at the character of Captain Wirz, as shown by official records that can to-day be found in every public library. Ask for "The War of the Rebellion Official Records of the Union and Confederate Armies," as published by the United States Government. Series 2, Vols. IV, V, and VIII, and Series 3, Vol. V, show that as soon as Captain Wirz went on duty at Andersonville his very first act was to try and better the condition of the prisoners, both as to rations and the sanitary surroundings of the prison and hospital, as the following letters to Capt. R. D. Chapman, Acting Adjutant of Post, Col. D. S. Chandler, Assistant Adjutant and Inspector-General, and others, show:

> "Headquarters Com. of Prison,
> "Camp Sumter, Andersonville, Ga.,
>> "June 6, 1864.

"Capt. R. D. CHAPMAN,
> "Acting Adjutant of Post.

"CAPTAIN: I must respectfully call the attention of the Colonel Commanding post, through you, to the following facts: The bread which is issued to the prisoners is of such inferior quality, consisting fully of one-sixth of husk, that it is almost unfit for use, and increasing dysentery and other bowel complaints. I would wish that the Commissary of the Post be notified to have the meal bolted or some other contrivance arranged to sift the meal before using it. If the meal, such as it is now, was sifted, the bread rations would fall short fully one-quarter of a pound. There is great deficiency of buckets; rations of rice, beans, vinegar and molasses can not be issued to the prisoners for want of buckets, about 8,000 men in the stockade being without anything of the sort. If my information is correct any number of buckets can be secured from Columbus, Georgia, if the quartermaster of the post would make requisition for the same.

"Hoping you will give this your attention as soon as possible,

"I remain, Captain, most respectfully, your obedient servant,

"H. WIRZ,

"Capt. Commanding Prison."

"Camp Sumter, Andersonville, Ga.,

"August 1, 1864.

"Colonel CHANDLER, C. S. A.

"COLONEL: I have the honor to enclose consolidated report of the military prison under my charge for the month of July, 1864. Allow me to point out some items which, if possible, ought to be attended to. We have an inadequate supply of tools to put the interior of the prison in a proper condition. We need axes, wheel-barrows, and other similar supplies. We need lumber, lime, iron and sheet-iron for baking pans. The prison, although a large addition has recently been made to it, is still too crowded. Almost daily large numbers of prisoners arrive, and before two weeks it will be in the same condition it was before the addition was made, and all internal improvements, which you are aware yourself are of the utmost importance, will come to a dead halt for the want of room.

"As long as 30,000 men are confined in any one inclosure the proper policing is altogether impossible. A long confinement has depressed the

spirits of thousands, and they are entirely indifferent. Manifold ways and means have been resorted to get out of the stockade. One prisoner
alone has made his escape through a tunnel. All
the others escaped from the guards while at work
on the outside.

"The rations are mostly the same as for our
own men, one-third of a pound of bacon, and one-
fourth pound of corn-meal, or one pound of fresh
beef in lieu of the bacon; occasionally beans, molasses, and rice are issued. Vinegar and soap,
both very important articles, are very seldom issued, as the commissary says he cannot get them.
Scurvy is the principal disease, and it and all other
diseases are in undue proportion to the old prisoners, who were at first at Richmond and Belle
Isle. The guard which I require for safe keeping
of the prisoners is entirely insufficient, simply because the men have to perform guard duty every
other day. This, it is not necessary for me to say,
is too much. With the exception of a portion of
the Fifty-fifth Georgia, the balance are militia-
men, and are undrilled and undisciplined. A good
deal could be said here as to how and why the
prison is not in a better condition, but I deem it
unnecessary, as you have seen for yourself where
the fault lies. Hoping your official report will
make such an impression with the authorities at
Richmond that they will issue the necessary orders
that will enable us to get what we so badly need,

"I remain, Colonel, most respectfully, your obedient servant,

"H. WIRZ,

"Capt. and Assistant Adjutant General
"Commanding Prison.

"Respectfully submitted with report.

"D. T. CHANDLER,

"Assistant Adjutant and Inspector-General."

CHAPTER X

THE FATE OF A TRAITOR

About the middle of August a heavy rain storm swept over the camp, the rain falling in sheets, and soon the small stream that ran through the camp was a raging torrent. It was so sudden and violent that in places it broke the stockade and in places within the inclosure it dammed up. The water came down the north and south slopes in floods, carrying with it filth and refuse. It was hard on the prisoners and it produced great suffering among us. On the other hand it was a blessing, as it carried off millions of vermin and freshened up the camp.

In many places the water concentrated and cut small channels on the way to the creek. This was particularly the case near the stockade between the north gate and the creek. At this place, about two hundred yards north of the creek and at an elevation of about fifteen feet above it, stood a large pine stump about six feet inside of the deadline, and the rapid flow of the water cut a channel about two feet deep and three feet wide along the west side and close to this stump; a strong flow of water cut its way down this channel during the storm. Great was the surprise and rejoicing the next morning when it was found that the channel had developed a vein of cold, pure water at the root of this stump, and the water proved to be a living spring.

Its source, as stated above, was six feet inside the dead-line, and we were furnished boards of which we made a trough about ten feet long to carry the water across the dead-line to us.

This was truly a God-send to the prisoners.

In all the reminiscences of my comrades that I have read, not one who speaks of this spring has given the true cause of its source or origin, and coming to us as it did I'll admit that it was providential, but it came in a natural way easily accounted for.

I visited Andersonville in 1902, and when I stepped off the train at the station (very much the same as it was in 1864) a boy ten cr eleven years of age introduced himself to me as a guide who "knew everything about the place, past and present." He was a bright youngster, and I engaged him at once to pilot me and to tell me everything about Andersonville. I said nothing to him about my ever having been there, and we started on our tour of inspection.

I had asked him only a few questions, when, I presume, wishing to exhibit his Sherlock Holmes qualities, he said: "You are from the nawth?" "Why, how did you know?" I inquired, and he repeated a few words I used in which the letter *r* predominated, and he said, "I could tell by your talk." I feigned surprise at his astuteness, which pleased him greatly.

This little fellow was a small walking encyclopedia of Andersonville knowledge. Many of the incidents he mentioned really had occurred, but others were a little apocryphal. "Providential Spring" was the leading attraction with my young guide, and he took me there first of all. He didn't begin his historical harangue until we came to the spring and had taken a drink and seated ourselves on the rude bench, when he said, "Many years ago there was a high stockade wall built around these grounds where there were thousands of people imprisoned, and during the late summer water became low in the creek down there and there was great suffering among the people; but there was one good man among them, and one day when the suffering was most intense this pious man knelt right down there, " – pointing to the opposite side from where we sat, – "and earnestly prayed to God to send water to relieve the sufferings of the prisoners, and when he arose to his feet water burst out right there from under the stump and it has been flowing ever since."

I found out afterward that this legend was accepted by a few of the young people and by all the negroes in that region.

Captain Wirz upon one occasion when speaking to me mentioned parole. This was before my comrades were taken to the hospital. It was to a certain extent a sort of reflection upon the character of a prisoner to accept a parole to do work in the prison and about it and to the interest of the enemy. I will confess the temptation to accept Wirz's invitation was trying, and will also confess that I afterward regretted not acting upon his suggestion. I think that I could have availed myself of the opportunity had it not been that my intimate friend, Sergeant Bowles, a high-minded, intellectual fellow, was so bitterly opposed to the idea in general. I do not think that I mentioned the suggestion made by Captain Wirz to him or to any of my comrades. The opportunity presented itself again; but as poor Bowles and I were the only ones of the original eleven left, and he was in feeble health, I couldn't bear to leave him and I concluded to stay with him to the last.

During the latter part of July several of the prisoners engaged in an attempt to dig a tunnel to freedom. Many of the prisoners knew of the plan and the greatest secrecy was observed. The work of tunneling was carried on at intervals during the dead of night. The progress of the work was well advanced when, on July 23, a rebel sergeant and a squad came in and stopped further operations. The excitement was intense, and many surmises and conjectures were made as to who the informer was.

I will quote from Mr. Urban for the purpose of correcting a mistake under which he evidently labored (See "Battlefield and Prison Pen," pp. 363 and 364):

"But the rebels discovered it [the tunnel] and had come into the prison for the purpose of shutting it up. The rebels intimated very plainly that they had received the information of its existence from one of our men, and it created a terrible excitement and anxiety to find out who the culprit was. Suspicion at last rested upon an Irishman known among us as 'Big Tom.' He was a man of immense stature, and was as good, honest, and warm-hearted a son of Erin as could be found anywhere. For some unaccountable reason a few of the prisoners suspected him of disclosing the tunnel to the rebels, and in a short time he was in the hands of an infuriated mob, who charged him with the crime. He earnestly denied the charge, but the maddened men would not listen to him or give him a chance to defend himself. A considerable number of those who believed Tom innocent gathered together and made an effort to get him out of the hands of the mob. After much trouble we succeeded in doing so, but not until the poor fellow was in a sad plight. His hair was cut off on one side of his head and he had received a terrible beating. One of the enraged men had struck him over the left eye with a stick of wood, inflicting a fearful wound. During the terrible trial he passed through, and when his life was in the most imminent danger, the brave Irishman kept as cool and collected as possible for any one to be under such circumstances; and, although protesting his innocence in the most earnest manner, he did not betray any indications of fear.

"After we succeeded in getting him away from his tormentors, he requested me to dress the wound on his face and clip the balance of his hair, 'so as to look more respectable,' as he expressed it.

"In a few hours after we had got Tom out of the hands of the mob, the excitement was renewed in the central part of the prison; and on going there I found that the prisoners, who had kept on hunting for the guilty party, had arrested another man on suspicion of disclosing the tunnel to the enemy. This time, however, they succeeded in getting the right one. His base conduct was found out from the fact that he had a considerable quantity of food and tobacco; and on being questioned in regard to where he received it, he could give no satisfactory answer, and his fear disclosed the fact that he was the guilty party. His demeanor was just the opposite of that of the one who was first arrested. His face was as pale as death, and his limbs shook with terror as he confessed that he was guilty of the deed, and he begged most piteously that his life might be spared. His captors had succeeded in getting possession of an old well rope, by which they intended to hang him in one of the wells; and they would have succeeded in accomplishing their object had not Wirz found out the state of affairs, and sent in a squad of men to rescue him. He was taken outside, but did not fare as well as the traitor who had disclosed the

10

first tunnel. Instead of protecting him and keeping him out of the prison, as they in honor were bound to do, Wirz had him sent back into prison again. He issued an order, however, before doing so, that he would stop our rations if we killed the traitor.

"The poor miserable wretch, almost dead with fright, was sent back to us again, where he knew that almost every one's hand would be turned against him. He did not live long after being sent back by the rebels. He was abused by some and shunned by all, and in a short time his body was carried to the dead-house."

This is true excepting that Captain Wirz had him sent back into prison. Mr. Urban is mistaken in this. The poor unfortunate wretch was from ten days to two weeks under the protection of the guards, and when he returned unexpectedly to the prison, whether of his own volition or otherwise, Captain Wirz was absent on sick leave, and had been away from the prison since about August 1.

There had been several attempts to escape by tunneling, and a few succeeded in getting away, but were either recaptured or killed in the attempt to regain their freedom.

Bloodhounds were employed by the authorities of the prison to pursue prisoners who had regained their freedom and were trying to get into the Union lines, or get beyond the precincts of this dismal prison.

CHAPTER XI

THAT TERRIBLE AUGUST

August was a terrible month at Andersonville. The heat was terrific and the fatality among the prisoners was something awful. Scurvy, the most destructive disease that afflicted us, was now fearfully prevalent. Nearly one-half the men were afflicted with it, and hundreds were dying daily. The first symptoms of the awful disease were generally a soreness of the gums, and shortly afterward ulceration set in, and unless the malady was checked the teeth became loose and fell out.

Lieutenant Davis was in command, and, I believe, did all he could with the scant supply of food and medicine at hand, to alleviate the condition.

Notwithstanding the derogatory reports relative to Wirz, I heard men say during that awful August, "I wish that Captain Wirz was back."

The reader, North and South, will concede that during the summer of 1864 the Southern Confederacy was on "its last legs." Its means of transportation was broken in many places and its food and clothing supplies meager and inadecuate. In fact, the whole South was in an impoverished condition.

Here was the same as a city with a population

of over 30,000 souls. Some writers put it at 35,-
000, but at the lowest there were 30,000 prisoners
at Andersonville in August, 1864. Imagine what
it was under the conditions in the South at that
time to provide food, scant though it was, for
those thousands.

It was said at Andersonville, and I have, during
the past fifteen or twenty years, read accounts from
Southern sources, that the Confederate Government during the summer of 1864 asked the Washington authorities to send physicians and hospital
supplies for the express use of Union prisoners
held in the South; they pledged that those supplies
would be only for the Union prisoners; and it
was said that the Washington authorities ignored
the proposition.

This seemed incredible, and I hoped that this
charge could be satisfactorily contradicted by
Northern writers acquainted with the facts, but
I have never read or heard a word in refutation
of it.

The rations issued to us in August were prin-
cipally corn meal, corn bread, peas, rice and bacon.

"A Yankee in Andersonville," an interesting
article written by T. H. Mann, M. D., which appeared in the *Century Magazine,* July, 1890, says,
"Corn bread and bacon were issued to us in fair
quantities." Dr. Mann was a prisoner at Andersonville at that time.

It is the fairest and most truthful account, brief
though it is, that I have ever read of Anderson-

ville. There is not a word about the apocryphal robbery of Union prisoners by rebel officers and guards, and not a word of the stereotyped and harrowing tale of Wirz's cruelty and rebel abuse. On the contrary, Dr. Mann says, "Our guard used us well, and I would say here that during our whole captivity we always experienced good usage from an old soldier."

In referring to a fellow-prisoner named Brown, Dr. Mann says, "He was the only man in the whole prison coming under my observation who did not seem affected by prison life. It did affect him, but in the form of a blessing rather than an evil. At the time of his arrival in the prison he was a mere brute crazed with whiskey; and his intellect, which was naturally strong, even brilliant, was nearly destroyed. After one month's abstinence he seemed stronger, healthier, and improved rapidly every day. His conversation, stories of his life, and brilliant qualities of mind were very entertaining to our immediate circle, and were of assistance toward keeping our spirits good. With all our suffering this man proved to us, beyond a doubt, that there was one condition in this world that a man might reach worse than Andersonville."

In regard to the corn beer, Dr. Mann says, "Several enterprising individuals commenced the manufacture of beer. They procured a keg in which would be placed four or five quarts of corn meal and as many gallons of water. After re-

maining in the hot sun for a day or two the mix-
ture would become very sour, then the keg would
be filled with water and the whole allowed to work
itself clear. It tasted good and was retailed at
five cents a glass. It was the only sour thing we
could get and it seemed to check the ravages of
scurvy."

I will be a little captious with Dr. Mann by re-
marking that he might have added that this effica-
cious beverage was introduced and brought into
use at Andersonville by Captain Wirz.

In the *Century Magazine* of November, 1890,
there appeared an article by J. T. King entitled,
"On the Andersonville Circuit."

Mr. King was a prisoner in Andersonville during the terrible summer of 1864. He suffered
with us, and he tells of his experience without any
bias, prejudice or bitterness. In this his article
shows a likeness to the latter-day histories of that
terrible prison. It is such a refreshing contrast to
those harrowing stories that had for twenty-five
years preceded it; those romances that portray
the Southerner and Confederate as an incarnate
demon. In the article Mr. King has not one derogatory or condemnatory word regarding Captain Henry Wirz.

Spencer, in his "Narrative of Andersonville" (p.
110), says that a poor sick prisoner begged Wirz
to permit him to step outside for fresh air, and
that "Wirz replied, 'Any air is too good for a
damned Yankee' and pulled out his revolver

and shot him down. The man died two hours afterward. Wirz, shooting him with his revolver, said, 'I am killing more Yankees at Andersonville than Lee is in front of Richmond.' "

Then again he tells of similar scenes which I refer to the reader; but it is all too harrowing, distressing, and unreasonable to reproduce. These are but a few of the many stories told by historian Spencer.

Why does not Sergt. J. T. King relate some of these wild-eyed stories in his article on Andersonville? Or why does not Dr. Mann? The answer is plain and simple. They are alleged incidents that never occurred.

We can however afford at this late day to be honest and tell the truth. The truth is sad and bad enough, and it is slowly rising though it has been crushed to earth for many years.

Sergeant King gives a little incident before his entry into the prison: "One elderly gentleman remarked, 'Yankees can't stand up against our Southern soldier. We whip them on every battlefield. Why, one of our boys –' 'Look heah, old man,' said one of our guards, 'I can't have you talking to these men like that; you never saw a Yank with a gun in his hands in your life. I tell you they are damned hard to catch! Now stand back.' "

And in his brief account of the "raiders" among us, Sergeant King says, "A portion of the prisoners were transformed into beasts and began to prey upon others. They snatched and ate the rations of the weaker ones. We called them 'raiders,' and they grew in number and boldness until murder was added to theft, and no one was safe. They made raids within a few steps of where I lay, and cut and bruised some men in a horrible manner."

He gives an account of the trial and execution of the six, but I was surprised that he gave no credit to Wirz for his assistance and cooperation in subduing them.

Mr. King also refers to the small-pox epidemic, but he has the fairness in referring to the general vaccination of prisoners to refrain from adding that monstrous charge of some of the early writers, to wit, that poison was mixed with the vaccine matter. Neither does Dr. Mann intimate such a thing, much less make the charge.

In speaking of the non-exchange of prisoners Sergeant King says, "Others swore and cursed. They cursed everybody related to the Confederacy and the things that had contributed to the hardships of their prison experience; and as if there were not material enough to curse on that side, they crossed the lines and even cursed Lincoln and Grant, because of the broken cartel."

Why Sergeant King excepts Secretary Stanton is something that I do not understand, for among the prisoners at Andersonville in August and September, 1864, Edwin M. Stanton shared as much or more cursing because of our detention than all others.

We might have been in the wrong to murmur against the policy of Secretary Stanton, not to "exchange skeletons for well-fed men," but it meant much to us and appeared a most cold-blooded verdict.

We should have emulated the patriotism of Thomas Cromwell, the ill-fated favorite of Henry VIII. When, after his sentence of death he received a courteous letter from the King, saying, "My dear, sweet Cromwell, it is my wish and pleasure that you should die without a murmur," he replied, "Tell my great and gracious sovereign that I cheerfully acquiesce."

I am afraid there were but few Cromwells at Andersonville. We were sufficiently human to fall in line with those of whom it was said, "The spirit was willing but the flesh was weak."

All the allegations that the rebels put obstacles in the way of exchange and deliberately chose to starve prisoners is certainly open to serious question, at least from my experience.

It was understood that we received about the same rations at Andersonville that were issued to the guards. This is supported by a letter written by a Union prisoner, confined at Andersonville, which appeared in the New York *Daily News* of August 9, 1865. The regrettable part about the thing is that he did not sign his name in full, only his initials, "M. S. H." It was believed, however, by soldiers at the time, or at least so reported, that after being paroled at Jacksonville, Florida, he rejoined his regiment, was promoted, and at the time that the letter was written he was an officer on General Sheridan's staff. This letter in part is as follows:

"Having been for several months an inmate of the stockade at Andersonville, I propose herein to consider, in the first place, the cause of the excessive mortality there; and secondly, how much of its frightful suffering is chargeable to Captain Wirz. The mortality at Andersonville resulted mainly from the following causes: (1) want of food, (2) want of shelter, (3) want of medical attendance and hospital diet, (4) causes of a purely local nature, coupled with the moral degradation exhibited by some of the prisoners themselves. By the want of proper food I mean the dietary scale was neither of the kind nor quality to which most of the prisoners had been accustomed. Still, it was the ordinary diet of the Confederate Army, and they had nothing else to give us. Thousands of the prisoners had never eaten bread made of corn meal or any preparation of it whatever; and with those its use commonly resulted in diarrhea, which, aggravated by the excessive use of water, generally in a few days became chronic. Every one knows the difficulty of treating this disease even under the most favorable circumstances. At first the meal was issued

uncooked and the prisoners were allowed to go
outside the stockade, under guard, in squads to collect fuel. This privilege was accorded with the
understanding that an escape would not be attempted. In a short time, however, Captain Wirz
was compelled to withdraw the favor, for it was
evident that no reliance could be placed on the
promises of some of the men.

"The cooks were our own men liberated from
the stockade for this special duty on parole, and
receiving therefor an extra ration and the liberty
of the entire post, with other privileges.

"As for the quantity of food, I know that until
Generals Sherman and Kilpatrick destroyed the
railroad communications of the South, the rations
as issued by post commissary was nearly if not
equal to that of our guards. * * *

"There are they whose portraitures have filled
our pictorials and upon whose testimony of suffering and starvation the conviction of Captain Wirz
will be sought, and whose vindictiveness now in
the hour of triumph, to which they contribute little
or nothing, is equalled only by their total want of
magnanimity, manhood, and self-control while
prisoners. Is he (Wirz) to be held up to the
world as a murderer of hitherto unknown magni-
tude? I trust not. In our national heraldry I see
an olive branch for the conquered, not a hangman's noose. Believe me, I have no personal interest or object in making this statement or appeal.
I never spoke to Captain Wirz or he to me."

The above is a brief, fair, and correct statement of the situation at Andersonville. "M. S. H." states facts.

As to the responsibility for the non-exchange of prisoners, I will here insert some official correspondence.

The following is an extract from a letter dated Washington, D. C., September 30, 1864, marked "confidential" and written to Maj. Gen. J. G. Foster, U. S. A., who had charge of exchange of prisoners at Hilton Head, South Carolina:

"Hereafter no exchange of prisoners shall be entertained except on the field when captured. Every attempt at special or general exchange has been met by the enemy with bad faith. It is understood that arrangements may be made later toward exchange of sick and disabled men on each side.

                    "H. W. HALLECK,
          "Maj. Gen. and Chief of Staff."

See page 895, Series II, Vol. VII, Official Records War of the Rebellion. Also, see on page 602 of the same volume:

          "City Point, Va., August 21, 1864.
"Hon EDWIN M. STANTON,
          "Secretary of War.

"Please inform General Foster that under no circumstances will he be authorized to make an exchange of prisoners of war. Exchanges simply reinforce the enemy at once, whilst we do not get the benefit for two or three months, and lose the majority entirely. I telegraph this from just hearing that some 500 or 600 more prisoners had been sent to General Foster.

> "U. S. GRANT,
> "Lieut. General."

In August Brigadier-Generals H. W. Wessells and T. Seymour were appointed to visit the South, looking into the treatment of prisoners of war.

The following are extracts of a lengthy report made by General Seymour, dated Williamstown, Mass., Aug. 10, 1864, and directed to Col. W. Hoffman, Commissary General of Prisoners, Washington, D. C.:

"The Southern authorities claim they give to prisoners precisely what the soldiers are allowed in the field. I believe this to be true of the rations, but of nothing else. The Southern soldier, even in his most prosperous days, lived simply upon corn and a bit of bacon, upon which he now is supported. Few Northern men, except in the almshouse, were ever reduced to the common rule of diet of the Southern race.

"The Southern authorities are exceedingly desirous of an immediate exchange of prisoners.

General Wessells and myself had an interview with General Ripley at Charleston, S. C., on this point. Their urgency is unbounded, but we asserted that it was the poorest possible policy for our Government to deliver to them 40,000 prisoners, better fed and clothed than ever before in their lives, in good condition for the field, while the United States received in return an equal number of men worn out with privations and neglect, barely able to walk, often drawing their last breath, and utterly unfit to take the field as soldiers.

"But this anxiety on the part of the rebels is one of the strongest possible proofs of the failing strength of their cause. Between Lee's and Hood's armies the country is a waste, redeemed only by the labor of the females, young and old, and the slaves. The last men have gone to the field of battle, and rather than to reinforce their army, as exchange would do, it was urged by our authorities that it would be much wiser to leave the prisoners where they are. * * *

"T. SEYMOUR,
"Brig. Gen. U. S. Vols."

The above appears in the same volume.

To show that there was suffering by prisoners on both sides and needless cruelty I will insert some correspondence of our officials:

"Office Commissary General of Prisoners,
   "Washington, D. C., August 12, 1864.
"Col. A. A. STEVENS,
   Commanding Camp Morton,
    "Indianapolis, Ind.

"COLONEL: The Surgeon-General has referred to this office a report from Surgeon C. J. Kipp, U. S. Vols., in charge of the hospital at Camp Morton, from which it appears that a variety of diseases are prevailing there of a more or less malignant character, owing to the crowded condition, which caused an unusually large fatality during the week ending July 24. Much of this is attributed to the want of anti-scorbutics, none of which have been issued since last fall. As the regulations provide for obtaining these articles there seems to be no sufficient reason why supply has not been procured to prevent diseases which are induced by their absence. All proper means should be used to guard against unusual sickness, by attention to diet or good state of police, and by not overcrowding in the camp. Is it not possible to enlarge the camp?

"Very respectfully, your obedient servant,
                  "W. HOFFMAN,
    "Col. Third Infantry, and
   "Commissary General of Prisoners."

Same record:

"Point Lookout, Md., April 22, 1864.

"Col. A. G. DRAPER, Com'g.

"SIR: In compliance with orders from you I hereby make the following statement in regard to the shooting of a prisoner of war at Point Lookout, by a sentinel of the guard: I was at the guard-house at the time the shot was fired. I heard the report, and immediately proceeded to where the report came from. I saw the sentinel who fired the gun. He told me that he had shot one of the prisoners for refusing to obey orders which he was instructed to enforce.

EDWIN C. GASKELL,

"Second Lieut., Thirty-sixth Inf., U. S. A., Lieut. of the Guard."

See page 384, Series II, Vol. VII, War of the Rebellion Official Records:

"Prisoners of War Hospital,

"Point Lookout, Md.,

"May 31, 1864.

"Col. HOFFMAN,

Commissary-General of Prisoners.

"COLONEL: I have the honor to acknowledge the receipt of your communication of the 29th of May, requesting the names and circumstances attending the shooting of prisoners of war, previous to the arrival of Colonel Draper, and after March

30, 1864. In reply I most respectfully submit the following report:

"First, Paul Thoroughgood, Private, Company C, Fourth N. C. Cavalry, shot April 18, 1864, about 9.30 p. m. (See accompanying report to provost marshal, April 19, 1864.)

"Second, Mark Lisk, Private, Company I, Sixtieth Tenn. Inf., shot while asleep in his tent, on the night of the 21st of April. These are the only cases that have come to my knowledge occurring during the time specified in your communication.

"Very respectfully, your obedient servant,
"JAMES H. THOMPSON,
"Surgeon U. S. Vols. in charge."

Official Records War of the Rebellion, p. 878, Series II, Vol VII –

"Headquarters, Elmira, N. Y.,
"Sept. 30, 1864.

"Respectfully forwarded to the Commissary-General of Prisoners.

"SIR: Drainage of camp is not good. There is a pond of stagnant water in the center, which renders camp unhealthy. This ought to be remedied. There is no reason why the camp should not be healthy. Many men in tents without floors or blankets. Barracks should be erected instead of tents. Hospital accommodations very insufficient.

11

Hospital mess-rooms much needed. Police of hospital good, except sinks; an offensive smell enters the tents from these. I doubt whether, with present mode of construction, this could be prevented. Scurvy prevails to a great extent; many deaths resulting therefrom. Few, if any, vegetables have recently been issued. Greater effort should be made to prevent scurvy.

"B. F. TRACY,

"Col. Comd'g One Hundred and Twenty-seventh N. Y. Vols."

Page 894, same record –

"Medical Director's Office,
"Baltimore, Md., October 14, 1864.

"Train of 1200 prisoners from Elmira, N. Y., arrived yesterday. Five died en route to this place, and one since arrival of train. Sixty unfit to travel.

"C. F. H. CAMPBELL,

"Surgeon, U. S. Vols., and Med. Inspector."

"The condition of these sixty men was pitiable in the extreme and evinces criminal neglect, and inhumanity on the part of the officers in making selection for the transfer.

"J. SIMPSON,

"Surgeon U. S. Army, Med. Director.
"Baltimore, Md., October 14, 1864."

Page 892 –

"Office, Commissary-General of Prisoners,
"Washington, D. C.

"Respectfully submitted to the Secretary of War.

"SIR: No precaution was taken to guard against unnecessary suffering by the prisoners ordered South, but from the within reports it appears that both the commanding officer and the medical officer not only failed to be governed by these orders, but neglected the ordinary promptings of humanity in the performance of their duties toward sick men, thus showing themselves to be wholly unfit for the positions they occupy, and it is respectfully recommended that they be immediately ordered to some other service.

"W. HOFFMAN,

"Col. Third U. S. Inf. and Com.-Gen. of Prisoners."

CHAPTER XII

BILLY BOWLES GIVES A DINNER IN BALTIMORE

In September there began a general movement of the prisoners from Andersonville. They went in detachments, many of them leaving during the first week of September, but "our party" did not leave the prison until the middle of the month. Those prisoners were sent further south to Millen, Savannah, and other points. It was, of course, understood that our Government had changed its mind in regard to exchange and all were buoyed up with new hope; it looked more like exchange of prisoners than it had at any time since we left Belle Isle.

Bowles, who walked with great difficulty with the aid of a stick, needed all the assistance I could give him. Our progress was slow to the depot, but the guards were kind, and finally about 1,000 of us were aboard the train. We started toward Macon.

It was a sad journey for Billy and I, since we had to leave so many of our comrades whom we had become attached to, and more particularly sad because we had to leave our nine home boys who were buried in the grave-yard; but we were going to be exchanged, so they said.

At the end of the third day we reached Savannah, and were turned into a pen built of boards about fifteen feet high in one of the public squares of the city.

This ended our dream of home and friends, and nearly knocked the remaining life out of us; however, it was a change for the better, for there were only about 5,000 prisoners here, and the sanitary condition was a great improvement on Andersonville.

I have a letter before me written to my sister, dated at this place, October 5, 1864, which, in part, is as follows:

"We were removed from Andersonville to this place about the middle of last month. I will not attempt to describe this prison life. Many thousands of our young men died at Andersonville during the past summer. Among them all my company boys who were captured with me over a year ago, except Bowles, of Company L, of the Seventh Cavalry, is still with me.

"The question is, must we all die? Is there no hope? Our Government has abandoned us! It appears that God is our only friend left I have for months been sustained by an abiding, undying hope that we would be exchanged 'next week,' but now that hope is gone.

"If our War Secretary don't act soon to save the remaining few, then, God forgive somebody!"

On October 12 we were put aboard the cars again and sent to Camp Lawton (Millen), which is situated about seventy-five miles from Savannah, at the junction of the Savannah and Macon Railroad. We were wholly in the dark as to where we were going, but we were not to wait long, for that same day we drew up in sight of a newly built stockade, situated very much as Andersonville was, and very much resembling that prison.

For some reason we were halted in front of the gate for quite a while. Our hearts sank within us; there was not a word spoken except the orders of the guard. "Well, Jim," whispered poor Billy Bowles, who stood at my side, "this settles it. Another winter in prison in our condition means death."

While standing there, who should come to us but Whitcomb, of Company L, one of our old Andersonville partners. It was a surprise indeed. He asked permission to speak to us and the answer was, "All right." We were glad to meet again. He had preceded us to Millen.

He told us that he was out on parole working at his trade. Whitcomb looked well and clean.

I asked him what the chances were for work outside of the prison. "Good," he replied, "for all who have a trade." "Then you must get me out. I am at the end of my rope. I love my country, but I love my own life a little more. I don't see how my death in prison will be of benefit to the Government." "I have been of that opinion, Jim, for lo these many moons. If Secretary Stanton or General Grant had a year's experience of corn meal and no clothing, I believe that they would experience a change of heart about this exchange business; but, Jim, surveying is a little slack, I think. What else can you do?" "Anything, recommend me for anything." "All right," he heartily rejoined, and left us.

We were soon after regularly "booked," and became inmates of Millen Prison.

There was a stream of good, pure water running through the camp, and our rations consisted of a pint of corn meal, about one-half cupful of cooked rice, and one-half pound of beef and a little salt every twenty-four hours.

Mr. Urban, the author of "Battlefield and Prison Pen," who, reached this prison October 22, says (p. 440, 441):

"Sick prisoners were thrown in here among us to die like dogs. Oh, who can sum up the villainy and crimes of the authors of the rebel brutality in these Southern hell-holes? Surely, God metes out punishment to man for his inhumanity to his fellows. These demons will have a fearful catalogue to answer for."

Pretty hard on somebody!

The third day after reaching Millen my name was called out in the prison, and I reported to a young Confederate officer, who introduced himself as Captain Asbury, saying that I was recommended to him as a shoemaker. "That's me," said I. He asked me if I wanted to go out and work at my trade. "Yes, sir." "All right, come with me." After passing the guard at the gate he asked me where I had learned my trade. "At Kalamazoo, Michigan," I said.

To show the extremity to which I was driven and the rashness of my reply I must digress to explain. When at an early age I was left an orphan, dependant upon relatives who were very much exercised as to what to do with me, or what I was good for. They bound me out first to a carpenter named Rolph. I didn't like the work and quit it. Then I was given to a doctor, who soon declared that I was not cut out for that profession. I was then sent to Kalamazoo, to a merchant tailor, a good friend of the family and a good man, named Horatio Failing. Mr. Failing was very good to me and made an earnest effort to teach me the tailoring trade, but I soon tired of it. I did not like the confinement. A man named Timothy Paige, across the street from Failing's store, wanted me to come to him and learn the shoemaking trade. He was continually joking me about its taking "nine tailors and a bull-dog to make a man."

One Saturday, when passing his shop, he called me in and showed me through his establishment, explaining everything, and he made me a proposition to stay with him until I was of age. "I believe," said he, "that you are now fully competent to make a pair of boots."

Mr. Paige was what we call in Montana a "josher," but I was too young to catch on, and I told him that I would begin shoemaking the following Monday. That night I told my sister, who was boarding at the Failing home attending school, what I had done, but she persuaded me to visit our other sister living near Grand Rapids, and I have never seen Timothy Paige since.

That conversation constituted my apprenticeship as a shoemaker.

I accompanied Captain Asbury to his quarters, where I signed a parole promising not to go over five hundred feet from the stockade without a pass; not to talk to the negroes, etc.; then he took me to a double cabin that was used for a shoeshop, and introduced me to the foreman as a shoemaker and told him to put me to work.

That mythological old character known as Dame Fortune seemed to smile on me at my first meeting with the young Captain. As luck would have it, I knew the foreman. He was a "saddler" of a New York regiment whom I knew as a fellow-prisoner at Andersonville.

After the Captain withdrew I said to the foreman, "See here, old fellow, I am no shoemaker; but see the condition I am in. I must do something or die. Give it to me gently on the start until I can catch on, and I will be your undying friend." He laughed and said, "You haven't got any of the best of me, for I am no shoemaker either; I am a saddler. You'll make it all right." He gave me a pattern for different size bottoms for soles and lifts, and a set of knives, and put me to work. Oh, this was easy, cutting from patterns. The work at this time I think saved my life.

In about a week we moved into a new large shop, and seventy-five shoemakers were put at work. The most of these were from Massachusetts regiments whose names Captain Asbury had on list for some time. They were nearly all first-class shoemakers.

Captain Asbury put me in charge of the sole-leather department, with two good shoemakers as my assistants. I got along nicely, but I was nearly naked, and some clothing was necessary.

Captain Asbury had as a cook a bright mulatto boy who was a natural-born trader. He carried on quite a traffic among his dark brethren, and I gave the boy some sole-leather in exchange for some new muslin flour sacks.

After the trade I returned to the shop and started a small fire in the fireplace in the end of the building, that by the light of the blaze I might examine my purchase and find a way of making a shirt for myself. I was surprised to find Captain Asbury's name on every one of the eight sacks. I hastily turned them all wrong side out, and after "cashing" five of them I was planning how to cut a shirt out of the other three, when Captain Asbury walked in. We had become well acquainted, and while we radically disagreed politically he had always treated me with the utmost courtesy. His words to me as he approached were, "Hello, Page, you are the fellow who is stealing my sacks, are you?" I threw him the sack and said, "All right, Captain, if it is yours I do not want it; I was thinking of making me a shirt. You see mine is about gone." He glanced at it and then at me, and handed it back, saying, "It is all right, Page."

It was about this time that Asbury noticed that my feet were bare, and he directed me to see the upper cutter and get from him the uppers and take soles from my department and make myself a pair of shoes. I thanked him and followed his directions.

With the help of others in our mess, who knew the trade, I soon had the shoes completed.

Next day I informed the Captain that the shoes were done and asked what would be the price. He said, "We sell them to citizens for $125 and to our soldiers for $75. You may have them at the army price." This knocked me out. I told him that I had no means for such a purchase as this. He answered, "I will allow you $2 a day while you are working at your trade." This contract looked too formidable, and as I declined to put them on till they were paid for the result was that I hung them up in the shop by my bunk. The following Saturday, through the agency of the Sanitary Commission, there came to the prisoners a supply of shoes, socks, caps, and blouses. I found difficulty in fitting myself with shoes out of this stock. Meanwhile, Asbury hailed me and said, "Why don't you draw a pair of shoes?" "They are too small," I said. "Draw a pair," he replied, "and I will trade the shoes you made for them." The exchange was soon made.

The next morning, Sunday, I proceeded a short distance from the shop, to a secluded spot on the bank of the creek, and after taking a bath I attired myself with this motley new suit, of shirt and pants cut out of the flour sacks with my penknife, and secured together with threads gathered from the raveled edges; shoes acquired in the manner above described, and a blouse, cap, and socks obtained from the Sanitary Commission. This suit was not very stylish, tested by the latest fashion-plates, but I never felt so well dressed before or since, as when I shed my old shirt and pants which had served me more than a year without change, and donned my new garments.

About the middle of November the Captain told me that there was an exchange agreed upon by which 10,000 sick and wounded prisoners would soon be sent to Savannah and thence down the river to our transports. "Don't you wish you were sick?" he said. "I am sick, Captain," was my reply, "and also my friend inside the stockade; you must let him go, too." "Well, your time will come soon." On the evening of November 19 he said to me, "To-morrow you and your friend can go. What is your friend's name?" "Bowles;

Sergeant Bowles." "All right, be ready in the morning. I will see to it that Bowles goes too." "Captain, this seems too good to be true; but I believe you and I shall never forget your kindness to me."

The next morning Captain Asbury asked me to go around to the main entrance of the stockade, and wait there, and he went in and brought out Billy Bowles. I joined them. The poor fellow was overjoyed. At the depot I said to Asbury, "Captain, I deceived you when I stated that I was a shoemaker; but, oh, I did so want to get out of the prison! You know the condition that I was in and you surely will say that I was justified. I am not a shoremaker and I hope that you will forgive me for the deception." "Oh, that is nothing. I looked in on you one evening and saw you sitting between a couple of men who were working on your shoes, while you were entertaining them with stories, and I came to the conclusion then that you were not very high in the profession," was his laughing rejoinder; "but you filled the bill all right, you did your work well."

We were finally ordered to board the train, and when I shook hands with him a brother would not have shown deeper emotion.

In my visit through the South a few years ago I made an earnest effort to find Captain Asbury, and at last I was informed that he died at Ogle-thorpe, Georgia, soon after the close of the war.

He was a good, kind-hearted, charitable man, a true friend in need.

We were run back to Savannah that evening, and in due time we found ourselves again in the same old stockade we had recently occupied, near the center of the city.

Next morning about 1,000 of us were marched to the wharf and went aboard the transport *R. E. Lee,* and started down the river. Bowles and I were sitting in the bow of the boat talking. Among other things I said, "Billy, I have a feeling that this means exchange." He shook his head and was full of doubts. Captain Asbury, the guards, and every one during the two days with whom we came in contact told us that we were to be exchanged, but it had for fourteen months been the same old, old story: "Cheer up, Yanks, don't get downhearted; you will shortly be exchanged."

It was very foggy when we left the wharf, but now the fog, like a heavy curtain, began to lift from the land and water.

All at once there appeared before us floating in the distance the stars and stripes from a number of vessels. The excitement among the prisoners knew no bounds. Sticks and crutches were thrown overboard, and men yelled and cried and laughed and sang in a most frenzied manner.

We ran alongside the steamer New York, and, under the directions of officers, filed around the cook's cabin, on the steamer, where six hardtack and a piece of boiled pork were given to each as he passed. The food was received with the most ravenous eagerness.

Bowles and I clung together, and when we reached the lower deck we sat beside each other to eat our United States rations. We had hardly seated ourselves when there was heard a loud noise and great disorder.

It appeared that some of the prisoners flanked to get double rations, and the officers aboard the vessel being powerless to prevent it, ordered the cook and his men to suspend issuing rations, and ordered the prisoners below, telling them that cooked rations were all out and that they must wait.

The officer in charge begged the men to be quiet, and assured them that they would soon have all they wanted; but nothing would do, they must have food at once. They finally compromised the matter by the leaders of the ex-prisoners giving the officers of the vessel fifteen minutes to get them rations. Two guards were placed over the hatch-way and the officers departed.

As soon as the specified time was up, the ex-prisoners charged the guards and drove them upon the deck. They broke open the hatch-way and secured the hardtack and barrels of pork and beef. The boxes and barrels were smashed open, and the scene that followed beggars description. Raw pork and hard tack were snatched up and spirited away in absurd quantities. Many of them ate their last supper that evening.

"Great God," said Bowles to me, "come to simmer it down, Jim, what beasts men are!"

Next morning four hundred of us were transferred to the steamer Northerner, which started for Annapolis.

When we were fairly out to sea, I leaned over the side of the steamer and looked out seaward, and a picture presented itself to me which had a familiar aspect, as one I had seen before. It was such as had appeared to me in a dream eleven months before, and it recalled the dream to mind.

On Belle Isle, about the middle of December, 1863, when rumors of an early exchange were rife, I dreamed that I was leaning over the side of a steamer, proceeding out to sea, the sailors all about me. In front of me, seaward, some two miles out, there was a brig under full canvas, and some distance this side of it was a smaller vessel rigged as a sloop, also under full sail. Both were moving parallel to us and opposite to the direction of the steamer. Close by the side of the steamer two large, fat-looking fish rose to the surface in play and then disappeared. "Oh, see those hogs!" I exclaimed. A sailor at my side said, "They are porpoises." This dream of Belle Isle was fulfilled in every minute particular on the morning when we steamed out from the Savannah River nearly one year later. This seemed the more remarkable to me, since I was little accustomed to travel on steamships and had never seen a porpoise.

On November 27 we arrived at Annapolis. We were put ashore, given a bath, had our hair cut, and were rigged out in new suits of blue. Ah, this was living again! Good rations, good bunks to sleep on, and clean clothes!

We remained at Annapolis about a week, and were given a thirty days' furlough, and the commanding officer sent me with a hundred men to Baltimore with an order on the paymaster for commutation of rations, also an order on the Baltimore & Ohio R. R. from Baltimore to Detroit.

At Baltimore I made the blunder of taking the men first to the paymaster. There I dressed them up in line and they received commutation for rations and clothing. Some of them had nearly two years rations due them.

My detachment were nearly all Michigan boys. I called them together and told them that I had an order for their transportation to Detroit, and for all of them to meet me at the depot at 2 o'clock that afternoon so I could give them their tickets. The only ones who turned up at the depot were Bowles and Bugler Johnson, of Company G of my regiment, who remained with me during the day.

I obtained the hundred tickets, and we remained at the station until 4 o'clock, waiting for the boys to come. I delivered but two of the tickets, viz., to Bowles and Johnson. The other ninety-seven

12

tickets I left with the ticket agent and went with
Bowles to dinner.

As we sat down at the restaurant, Bowles took
from an inside pocket a ragged, discolored memorandum book, and handed it to me. It was the
bill of fare of the Christmas dinner that we did
not get at Belle Isle in 1863. I had forgotten
about it, but Billy had not. He motioned to a
waiter and said, handing him the memorandum
containing the menu, "I want that dinner dished
up for eleven." The waiter demurred to some of
the items, such as plum-pudding, but Billy was in-
exorable. The program must be carried out to
the letter, and for eleven. The waiter expected
that nine others would put in an appearance, and
gave the order. I expostulated with Bowles about
the ridiculousness of the thing, but he could not be
dissuaded from his purpose and an elaborate and
sumptuous repast, exactly as the menu stated, was
served.

My remonstrances were futile, and when the
waiter understood the situation he thought, I presume, that he had an insane man to deal with.

"We entered into a compact that Christmas
evening," said Bowles, "and I'm determined to
carry it out to the letter."

Every one of the eleven plates was filled with
good things, and except Billy's orders to the
waiter, hardly a word was spoken. It was the sad-
dest meal that I ever sat down to.

After leaving the restaurant Billy said, "When
I proposed to treat the boys to a Christmas dinner

I was sure that we would all be soon exchanged and that the programme would all be fully carried out; I didn't think it possible but that the Government would take action looking toward a speedy exchange, and that we would all be together to enjoy the dinner."

The next morning Sergeant Bowles, Bugler Johnson, and myself, the only ones out of the hundred, took the train for Detroit.

I remained with my relatives sixty days (my furlough having been extended thirty days on account of sickness), and then after being held at Harper's Ferry with about three hundred and sixty of my regiment for some time, during which we participated in the search for Booth, the murderer of our lamented Lincoln, I finally joined my company after an absence of about nineteen months. We participated in the Grand Review at Washington, and I was promoted to second lieutenant on the 23d day of May, 1865, and was mustered out of service on the 21st day of June, 1865, at Fort Leavenworth, Kansas.

As early as the spring of 1862, when the seceded States were blockaded by sea, and cut off by invading armies by land, it was plain that the Confederate Army and the people of the South would soon be in distress for the necessaries of life, for they would be wholly dependent on what could be raised in their country and there would soon be no one left to till the soil but the remaining slaves and the women and children.

I hold that if our Washington authorities had given the matter the consideration that the great subject demanded, they would have realized the importance of *early* exchange to save the lives of those so unfortunate as to be taken prisoners. If an immediate or early exchange had been agreed upon, which would have been as fair for one side as the other, there would have been no Andersonville Prison; the rows of marble slabs witnessing the graves of 13,000 or more of our young men in the National Cemetery at that place would not be there and the "we will not exchange able-bodied men for skeletons" policy would have been no excuse.

Our Government knew the destitute condition of the South and the consequence that would result if we were not early exchanged. This knowledge is my reason for making the charge that our Government must share the responsibility. The Government knew and did not act. While I never said anything about it while a prisoner and very little since, I felt that our Government was making a very serious blunder, in which thousands of lives were involved, and one that must sooner or later be recognized.

During those terrible days at Andersonville in the summer of 1864, when the condition of the prisoners had reached the state of invalidism and helplessness, the Government was confronted with a serious problem. I do not believe a general exchange at that time would have prolonged the strife a day.

PART II

HENRY WIRZ: THE MAN AND HIS
TRIAL

CHAPTER I

THE FACTS OF WIRZ'S LIFE

Major Henry Wirz, C. S. A., was born at Zurich, Switzerland, in 1822. He was the son of Abraham Wirz, an honest, respectable citizen of that city. After graduating at the University of Zurich, Henry Wirz took up the study of medicine, and to fit himself for his profession he attended the medical colleges of Paris and Berlin; in both of which schools he received the degree of M. D. He began the practice of medicine near his home, and soon after, while quite young, married. After giving birth to two children, his wife died, and Dr. Wirz decided to try his fortune across the sea.

Leaving his children with his father and mother, he immigrated to the United States. His father was in good circumstances financially, and the Doctor's children, Paul and Louisa Emily Wirz, had a good home. They remained in Switzerland, and both were living a few years ago.

Dr. Henry Wirz came to this country in 1849. He was a learned and skilful physician, and began the practice of his profession in Kentucky. Early in 1854 he married Mrs. Wolfe, a woman of good family, a widow, the mother of two little girls,

Susie and Cornelia Wolfe. The marriage took place at Cadiz, Kentucky, and was a happy one, as they were very much attached to each other. He was an affectionate husband and the kindest of fathers to his little step-children. February 25, 1855, a little girl came to cement more closely the bonds of affection between this loving pair. They named her Cora.

This was the only child of Major Wirz's last marriage and her life has been a most sad one. She was but ten years old when her father was executed at Washington. She well remembers the agonizing grief of her mother during that awful November of 1865, and how she begged for the body of her husband and was refused it by the authorities. They bluntly informed the weeping woman that she could not have the remains; that they had concluded to bury the body by the side of Mrs. Surratt and Herold, the "Lincoln conspirators," in the prison-yard. This was done.

It seems incredible at this time that men could be found on top of the earth that would have the heart to refuse such a request!

Major Wirz's youngest child is still living – Mrs. J. S. Perrin, of Natchez, Mississippi. She is the mother of three children living – Samuel Paul Perrin, Roscoe Wirz Perrin, and Miss Mary Gladys Perrin, and a few years ago she buried a beautiful daughter, Miss Maude Perrin.

After his second marriage Dr. Wirz removed to Milliken's Bend, Louisiana.

At the beginning of the Civil War he had a large and lucrative practice as a physician in the locality in which he lived.

In refutation of the many accounts by Andersonville historians of his being an "ignorant, uneducated person," I can say that I know from personal observation that he spoke English, German, and French.

When the war broke out he espoused the side of the South, and on June 16, 1861, he enlisted in Company A, Fourth Battalion, Louisiana Volunteers. This was a select military organization that did excellent service on the field of battle, particularly in 1861 and 1862. It was composed of as brave soldiers as ever faced an enemy. The members of this regiment acquitted themselves gallantly at Seven Pines. In this battle sergeant Henry Wirz was severely wounded, his right arm being badly shattered by a ball, and he never regained the use of it. The arm was so useless to him that while in command at Andersonville he learned to write with his left hand. During his trial in September and October, 1865, he was suffering from this wound.

He was in the hospital for some weeks after being wounded. After partially recovering he rejoined his regiment and was promoted to a captaincy, June 12, 1862, "for bravery on the field of battle." He was suffering from the wound that he received at the battle of Seven Pines, which unfitted him for duty at the front, and shortly after he was detailed as acting adjutant-general to Gen. J. H. Winder.

On August 26, 1862, Captain Wirz was placed in charge of the military prison at Richmond, Virginia, where he remained on duty till September 26, 1862, when he was ordered to Montgomery, Alabama, in search of missing records pertaining to prisoners captured in 1861 and the early part of 1862, and to report the result to Col. Robert Ould, Agent for Exchange.

After completing his work there to the satisfaction of his superiors, he was ordered by General Winder to repair to Tuscaloosa, Alabama, to take charge of the prison at that point.

His health failing him he applied for a furlough, and was directed to proceed to Richmond, Virginia. While there he was appointed a special plenipotentiary by President Davis on a mission to Paris and Berlin, and sailed for Europe the latter part of 1862.

While at Paris he had his wounded arm operated on, and, as the physicians supposed, all the diseased bone was removed. As he began to regain his health it was thought that the operation was a successful one; but this was not the case, for after completing his mission at Berlin the old trouble came back, and when he returned from Europe in February, 1864, he was suffering as much as ever.

In April, 1864, he was directed to report to Colonel Persons in command of the prison at Andersonville, Georgia, and to take charge of the interior of the prison. The date of the order was April 12, 1864.

When the war was closed in April, 1865, Captain Wirz was still at Andersonville. His wife, his little daughter, and his step-children were with him. He was suffering from his wound and was nearly impoverished. It was understood that he was included in the surrender of General Johnston and his forces to General Sherman.

Union troops were sent into Georgia at this time under command of General Wilson. This officer established his headquarters at Macon. On May 7, General Wilson sent Capt. H. E. Noyes, of the Fourth Regular Cavalry, to Andersonville with a squad of soldiers. They called on Captain Wirz, who had, during the winter preceding, been promoted to the rank of major.

Captain Noyes demanded the records of the prison, and Major Wirz collected them and handed them to him.

"I have been directed, Major," said Captain Noyes, "by General Wilson to take you to his headquarters."

"Very well, sir, I have no objection; but before we go, had you not better have something to eat. We have but little in the house, but, little or much, you and your men are welcome to it."

The Captain thanked him, and they sat down with the Wirz family to bread and bacon. Major

Wirz apologized for having no coffee or tea in the house.

As they were about to leave the house, Mrs. Wirz became very much agitated, and the little ones began to cry, but Major Wirz cheerfully assured them that no harm could come from his trip to General Wilson's headquarters. Mrs. Wirz said afterward that Captain Noyes's attitude made her uneasy from his first entrance into the house. There was something ominous in his stern looks and his silent demeanor. Except to thank Major Wirz when he suggested that they should wait to have dinner, he never uttered a word while the humble repast was being prepared nor when her husband was quieting her fears.

It was the last time that his little ten-year-old daughter, now Mrs. J. S. Perrin, saw her father.

Major Wirz was taken to Macon. After the party in command of Captain Noyes reached that city they immediately went to General Wilson's headquarters. The latter questioned Wirz at considerable length, and carefully examined the prison records. In the course of about two hours the General told him that that was all he wanted and that he could return to his family. Major Wirz bid the General good-by, and went to the depot to take the cars for Andersonville. The train was a few hours late, and after waiting at the depot for more than an hour, an officer with a few soldiers from General Wilson's headquarters came to the station and arrested Major Wirz and put him under guard.

A few days later he was sent to Washington, and placed in the Old Capitol Prison on May 10, 1865.

From that date until the following August, not only the Adjutant General's office, but the whole War Department were busy collecting evidence against the prisoner. Col. E. D. Townsend, Assistant Adjutant-General, was more than alert in gathering testimony. He figured very prominently in the prosecution, but, strange to say, in his memoirs recently published *there does not appear one word relative to Wirz or the trial*. This is significant.

CHAPTER II

THE ACCUSATIONS AGAINST WIRZ

The long delayed trial was initiated by the issuance of the following order:

"Special Order, No. 453.

"War Department,
"Adjutant General's Office,
"Washington, D. C., Aug. 23, 1865.

"A special Military Commission is hereby appointed to meet in this city at 11 o'clock A. M. on the 23d day of August, 1865, or as soon thereafter as practicable, for the trial of Henry Wirz, and such other prisoners as may be brought before it.

"Detail of the commission:

"Maj.-Gen. L. Wallace, U. S. Volunteers.

"Brev't Maj.-Gen. L. Thomas, Adjutant Gen., U. S. A.

"Brev't Maj.-Gen. G. Mott, U. S. Volunteers.

"Brig.-Gen. Francis Fessenden, U. S. Volunteers.

"Brig.-Gen. A. S. Bragg, U. S. Volunteers.

"Brev't Brig.-Gen. John F. Ballior, U. S. Volunteers.

"Brev't Col. T. Allcock, 4th N. Y. Artillery.

"Lieut.-Col. J. H. Stibbs, 12th Iowa Volunteers.

"Col. N. P. Chipman, Additional Aide-de-Camp, Judge-Advocate of the Commission, with such assistants as he may select, with the approval of the Judge-Advocate-General.

"The Commission will sit without regard to hours.

"By order of the President of the United States.

"E. D. TOWNSEND,
"Assistant Adjutant-Gen."

The specifications were as follows:

"SPECIFICATION I.

"In this that the said Henry Wirz, an officer in the military service of the so-called Confederate States of America, at Andersonville, in the State of Georgia, on or about the eighth day of July, A. D. 1864, then and there being commandant of a prison there located by the authority of the so-called Confederate States for the confinement of prisoners of war taken and held as such from the armies of the United States of America, while acting as said commandant, feloniously, wilfully, and of his malice aforethought, did make an assault, and he, the said Henry Wirz, a certain pistol called a revolver then and there loaded and charged with gunpowder and bullets, which said pistol the said Henry Wirz, in his hand then and

there held, to, against, and upon a soldier belonging to the army of the United States, in his, the
said Henry Wirz's custody as a prisoner of war,
whose name is unknown, then and there feloniously, and of his malice aforethought, did shoot
and discharge, inflicting upon the body of the soldier aforesaid a mortal wound with the pistol
aforesaid, in consequence of which said mortal
wound, murderously inflicted by the said Henry
Wirz, the said soldier, to wit, on the ninth day of
July, A. D. 1864, died."

And of thousands of prisoners who were at Andersonville on July 8 and 9, 1864, no one could
be found who knew the name of this man!

All the particulars attending the shooting and
death of the murdered man were minutely described upon oath at the trial except his name!

"SPECIFICATION 2.

"In this that the said Henry Wirz, an officer in
the military service of the so-called Confederate
States of America, at Andersonville, in the State
of Georgia, on or about the 20th day of September, A. D. 1864, then and there being commandant of a prison there located by the authority of
the said so-called Confederate States of America,
while acting as commandant, feloniously, wilfully,
and of his malice aforethought, did jump upon,
stamp, kick, bruise, and otherwise injure with the

heels of his boots, a soldier belonging to the army
of the United States in his, the said Henry Wirz's,
custody as a prisoner of war, *whose name is unknown,* of which said stamping, kicking, and bruising, maliciously done and inflicted by the said
Wirz, he, the said soldier, to wit, on the 20th day
of September, A. D. 1864, died."

They knew all the particulars, even the day that
he died, but they *didn't know his name.*

"SPECIFICATION 3

"In this that the said Henry Wirz, an officer
in the military service of the so-called Confederate
States of America, at Andersonville, in the State
of Georgia, on or about the thirteenth day of
June, A. D. 1864, then and there being commandant of a prison there located by the authority
of the so-called Confederate States of America,
while acting as said commandant, feloniously, and
of his malice aforethought, did make an assault,
and he, the said Henry Wirz, in his hand then
and there held, to, against, and upon a soldier
belonging to the army of the United States, in his,
the said Henry Wirz's custody as a prisoner of
war, *whose name* is *unknown,* then and there
feloniously, and of his malice aforethought, did
shoot and discharge, inflicting upon the body of
the soldier aforesaid a mortal wound with the

13

pistol aforesaid, in consequence of which said mortal wound, murderously inflicted by the said Henry Wirz, the said soldier immediately, to-wit, on the day aforesaid, died."

Notwithstanding the tedious monotony of these specifications and their sameness, I propose to set them down here *verbatim et literatim.*

I was at Andersonville, a prisoner, from February 27 to September 20, 1864, and while there I never heard nor never knew that Captain Henry Wirz was personally responsible for the death of a solitary prisoner, and I thought that I knew about everything that occurred there. There were thousands of us there and you can imagine how we discussed pro and con everything that took place; in fact, that was about all we had to do. You can also imagine what a topic for discussion the murder of a prisoner by Wirz would produce.

"SPECIFICATION 4

"In this that the said Henry Wirz, an officer in the military service of the so-called Confederate States of America, at Andersonville, in the State of Georgia, on or about the 30th day of May, A. D. 1864, then and there being commandant of a prison there located by the authority of the said so-called, Confederate States of America, for the confinement of prisoners of war taken and held as such from the armies of the United States of

America, while acting as such commandant. feloniously, and of his malice aforethought, did make
an assault, and he, the said Henry Wirz, a certain
pistol called a revolver then and there loaded and
charged with gunpowder and bullets, which said
pistol the said Henry Wirz, in his hand then and
there held, to, against, and upon a soldier belonging to the army of the United States, in his, the
said Henry Wirz's custody as a prisoner of war,
whose name is unknown, then and feloniously and
of his malice aforethought, did shoot and discharge, inflicting upon the body of the soldier
aforesaid a mortal wound with the pisto. aforesaid, in consequence of which said mortal wound
immediately inflicted by the said Henry Wirz the
said soldier, on the 30th day of May, A. D. 1864,
died."

Not the slightest whit of particulars wanting
except the name of the murdered man.

"SPECIFICATION 5

"In this that the said Henry Wirz, an officer
in the military service of the so-called Confederate
States of America, at Andersonville, in the State
of Georgia, on or about the 20th day of August,
A. D. 1864, then and there being commandant of
a prison there located by the authority of the so-
called Confederate States for the confinement
of prisoners of war taken and held as such from

the armies of the United States of America, while
acting as said commandant, feloniously, and of his
malice aforethought, did confine and bind with an
instrument of torture called 'the stocks' a soldier
belonging to the army of the United States, in his,
the said Henry Wirz's custody as a prisoner of
war, *whose name is unknown,* in consequence of
which said cruel treatment, maliciously and murderously inflicted as aforesaid, he, the said soldier,
to-wit, on the 30th day of August, A. D. 1864,
died."

I am confident that during the month of August,
1864, Captain Wirz was absent on sick leave and
that Lieutenant Davis was in command at Andersonville.

"SPECIFICATION 6

"In this that the said Henry Wirz, an officer
in the military service of the so-called Confederate
States of America, at Andersonville, in the State
of Georgia, on or about the first day of February,
A. D. 1864, then and there being commandant of
a prison there located by the authority of the so-
called Confederate States for the confinement of
prisoners of war taken and held as such from the
armies of the United States of America, while acting as commandant, feloniously and of his malice
aforethought, did confine and bind with an instrument of torture called 'the stocks' a soldier belonging to the army of the United States, in his, the

said Henry Wirz's custody as a prisoner of war, *whose name is unknown,* in consequence of which said cruel treatment, maliciously and murderously inflicted as aforesaid, he, the soldier, to wit, on the sixth day of February, A. D. 1864, died."

This man lived five days after Wirz's cruel treatment, and yet no one learned his name! Again, *Captain Wirz was not in command* at Andersonville at that time. Colonel Persons was in command. Captain Wirz did not reach Andersonville *till about April 12, 1864,* and yet this was a portion of the testimony that convicted him.

"SPECIFICATION 7

"In this that the said Henry Wirz, an officer in the military service of the so-called Confederate States of America, at Andersonville, in the State of Georgia, on or about the 20th day of July, A. D. 1864, then and there being commandant of a prison there located by the authority of the said so-called Confederate States for the confinement of prisoners of war taken and held as such from the armies of the United States of America, while acting as such commandant, feloniously did fasten and chain together several persons, soldiers belonging to the army of the United States in his, the said Henry Wirz's custody as prisoners of war, *whose names are unknown,* binding the necks and feet of said soldiers closely together and compelling them

to carry great burdens, to-wit, large iron balls
chained to their feet, so that, in consequence of the
said cruel treatment inflicted upon them by the
said Henry Wirz as aforesaid, one of said soldiers,
a prisoner of war as aforesaid, *whose name is unknown,* on the 25th day of July, A. D. 1864,
died."

The credulity of the Judge-Advocate was indeed marvelous! Is it not singular that he did not
insist at the trial that the name of at least one of
those "unknown" be produced? Not a name of
one of those victims was given at the trial.

"SPECIFICATION 8

"In this that the said Henry Wirz, an officer
in the military service of the so-called Confederate
States of America, at Andersonville, in the State
of Georgia, on or about the 15th day of May,
A. D. 1864, then and there being commandant of
a prison there located by the authority of the so-
called Confederate States, for the confinement of
prisoners of war taken and held as such from the
armies of the United States of America, while acting as said commandant, feloniously, wilfully and
of his malice aforethought, did order a rebel
soldier, whose name is unknown, then on duty as
sentry or guard to the prison of which the said
Henry Wirz was commandant as aforesaid, to
fire upon a soldier belonging to the army of the

United States in his, the said Henry Wirz's, custody as a prisoner of war, *whose name is unknown;* and in pursuance of said order so as aforesaid, maliciously and murderously given as aforesaid, he, the said rebel soldier, did, with a musket loaded with gunpowder and bullet, then and there fire at the said soldier so as aforesaid held as a prisoner of war, inflicting upon him a mortal wound with the musket aforesaid, of which he, the said prisoner, soon thereafter, to-wit, on the day aforesaid, died."

The shooting was alleged to have been done in the broad light of day in the presence of thousands, but none could give the name of the man.

"SPECIFICATION 9

"In this that the said Henry Wirz, an officer in the military service of the so-called Confederate States of America, at Andersonville, in the State of Georgia, on or about the first day of July, A. D. 1864, there and then being commandant of a prison there located by the authorities of the said so-called Confederate States for the confinement of prisoners of war taken and held as such from the armies of the United States of America, while acting as said commandant, feloniously and of his malice aforethought, did order a rebel soldier, whose name is unknown, then on duty as sentinel or guard to the prison of which the said Wirz was commandant as aforesaid, to fire upon a soldier belonging to the army of the United States, in his, the said Henry Wirz's, custody as a prisoner of war, *whose name is unknown;* and in pursuance of said order so as aforesaid, maliciously and murderously given as aforesaid, he, the said rebel soldier, did, with a musket loaded with gunpowder and bullet, then and there fire at the said soldier so as aforesaid held as a prisoner of war, inflicting upon him a mortal wound with the said musket, of which he, the said prisoner, soon thereafter, to-wit, on the day aforesaid, died."

"SPECIFICATION 10

"In this that the said Henry Wirz, an officer in the military service of the so-called Confederate States of America, at Andersonville, in the State of Georgia, on the 20th day of August, A. D. 1864, then and there being commandant of a prison there located by the authority of the so-called Confederate States for the confinement of prisoners of war taken and held as such from the armies of the United States of America, while acting as said commandant, feloniously, and of his malice aforethought, did order a rebel soldier, *whose name is unknown,* then and there on duty as sentinel or guard to the prison of which the said Henry Wirz was commandant as aforesaid, to fire upon a soldier belonging to the army of the United States, in his, the said Henry Wirz's, custody as a prisoner of war, *whose name* is *unknown*, and in pursuance of said order so as aforesaid, maliciously and murderously given as aforesaid, he, the said rebel soldier did, with a musket loaded with gunpowder and bullet, then and there fire at said soldier as aforesaid held as a prisoner of war, inflicting upon him a mortal wound, with the said musket, of which he, the said prisoner, to-wit, on the day aforesaid, died."

Notwithstanding the fact that Captain Wirz at this time was on sick leave, the findings of the court was "guilty" upon this specification.

"SPECIFICATION 11

"In this that the said Henry Wirz, an officer in the military service of the so-called Confederate States of America, at Andersonville, in the State of Georgia, on or about the first day of July, A. D. 1864, then and there being commandant of a prison there located by the authorities of the so-called Confederate States for the confinement of prisoners of war taken and held as such from the armies of the United States of America, while acting as said commandant, feloniously, and of his malice aforethought, did cause, incite, and urge certain ferocious and blood-thirsty animals called bloodhounds to pursue, attack, wound and tear in pieces a soldier belonging to the army of the United States in his, the said Henry Wirz's, custody as a prisoner of war, *whose name is unknown,* and in consequence thereof, the said bloodhounds did then and there, with the knowledge, encouragement, and instigation of him, the said Henry Wirz, maliciously and murderously given by him, attack and mortally wound the said soldier, in consequence of which said mortal wound he, the said prisoner, soon thereafter, to-wit, on the sixth day of July, A. D. 1864, died."

All the particulars, notice, are given and testified to except the man's name. The prisoner lived six days after being mangled by the bloodhounds, and yet no one ascertained his name!

"SPECIFICATION 12

"In this that the said Henry Wirz, an officer in the military service of the so-called Confederate States of America, at Andersonville, in the State of Georgia, on or about the 27th day of July, A. D. 1864, then and there commandant of a prison located by the authority of the so-called Confederate States for the confinement of prisoners of war taken and held as such from the armies of the United States, while acting as said commandant, feloniously, and of his malice aforethought, did order a rebel soldier, whose name is unknown, then on duty as sentinel or guard to the prison of which the said Henry Wirz was commandant as aforesaid, to fire upon a soldier belonging to the army of the United States, in his, the said Henry Wirz's, custody as a prisoner of war, *whose name is unknown,* and in pursuance of said order so as aforesaid, maliciously and murderously given as aforesaid, he, the said rebel soldier, did, with a musket loaded with gunpowder and bullet, then and there fire at said soldier so as aforesaid held as a prisoner of war, inflicting upon him a mortal wound with the said musket, of which said mortal wound he, the said prisoner, soon after, to-wit, on the day aforesaid, died.

"SPECIFICATION 13

"In this that the said Henry Wirz, an officer in the military service of the so-called Confederate States of America, at Andersonville, in the State of Georgia, on the 3rd day of August, A. D. 1894, then and there being commandant of a prison there located by the authority of the so-called Confederate States of America, for the confinement of prisoners of war taken and held as such from the armies of the United States of America, while acting as said commandant, feloniously, and of his malice aforethought, did make an assault upon a soldier of the United States in his, the said Henry Wirz's, custody as a prisoner of war, *whose name is unknown,* and with a pistol called a revolver, then and there held in the hands of the said Henry Wirz, did beat and bruise said soldier upon the head, shoulders, and breast, inflicting thereby mortal wounds, from which said beating and bruising and mortal wounds caused thereby, the said soldier, on the fourth day of August, A. D. 1864, died.

"By order of the President of the United States.
"N. P. CHIPMAN,
"Colonel, A. A. D. C. Judge-Advocate."

(In the above specifications I have italicized the "whose name is unknown.")

These were the charges upon which Major Henry Wirz, C. S. A., was tried, condemned, and hanged. His counsel filed pleas in bar to the charges and Wirz pleaded "not guilty."

1st. That he had been offered protection by Gen. J. H. Wilson, that he should not be held a prisoner.

2nd. He denied the jurisdiction of the court to try him.

3rd. That the war being ended and civil law restored, there was no military law under which he could be tried.

4th. He moved to quash the charges for vagueness as to time, place and manner of offense.

5th. He claimed a discharge, because as an officer in the Confederate Army he was entitled to the terms agreed to between Generals Sherman and Johnston upon the surrender of the latter.

The pleas being overruled, he pleaded "not guilty" to all the charges.

CHAPTER III

THE TRIAL

Everything being in readiness, the case was called August 25, 1865.

Col. N. P. Chipman, U. S. A., Judge-Advocate, had charge of the prosecution, with an array of assistants. Louis Schade, a fellow-countryman of Wirz, was the attorney for the defense. It appeared that Colonel Chipman had, from the start, everything his own way.

There were one hundred and sixty witnesses for the Government. Nearly all of these had been prisoners at Andersonville.

The banner witness for the prosecution was a bright, handsome Andersonville prisoner who gave his name as Felix de la Baume, and his birth place in eastern France, near the Rhine. He was of good address, pleasant-voiced, and intelligent. He saw the most of the killing attributed to the prisoner. His omnipresence while at Andersonville seemed something bordering on the supernatural. Nothing escaped him. Witness de la Baume held the surging crowd like an inspiration. His grip on the Northern ear was a secure one, as he glibly recounted the numerous and manifold cruelties of Henry Wirz. He captured the court.

Everything he said was believed and nothing was too heavy for his recital. Among other things of interest that he related was the statement, made without batting an eye, that the Marquis de Lafayette, Washington's friend and the hero of the battle of Brandywine, was his grand-uncle.

On the 19th of October, before the taking of the testimony was concluded, he was appointed to a position in the Department of the Interior.

Byron has said, "Time, alas, sets all things even." In this case Time didn't wait very long, for on November 21, only eleven days after Major Wirz's execution, de la Baume's official career came suddenly to an end. Some of the German soldiers at Washington recognized in Monsieur, the grand-nephew of Lafayette, a deserter from the Seventh New York Volunteers, whose name was not de la Baume, but plain Felix Oeser, and who was born in Saxony on the other side of the Rhine. Secretary of the Interior Harlan summarily dismissed Felix de la Baume-Oeser and Washington society knew him no more.

For the three months that Wirz languished in jail, before the trial, the radical press of the North was holding him up to the world as the greatest criminal of ancient or modern times. He was portrayed as a fiend, a demon, and a very monster in human shape. Attorney Louis Schade volunteered to defend Wirz, and when this became known he was ridiculed and lampooned by the press from Boston to Boise.

Major Wirz was so feeble, and suffering so much from his old wound, that he was unable to sit or stand, and a sofa was brought into the courtroom for him to recline on. This was another cause for an outburst from the press. He was charged with "shamming" to gain sympathy.

The fact seemed to be demonstrated at the trial that those who were the most favored at Andersonville were the best witnesses for the Government. It was a few of these witnesses that testified that Wirz was guilty of murder that convicted him, and the commission in its findings could not ignore the testimony.

Out of the one hundred and sixty prisoners at Andersonville who were witnesses, only ten or twelve testified to cruelty on the part of the commandant!

I was sorely disappointed in not being a witness at the trial, as I expected to be, for I had been notified that I would be called. But for some reason I was not.

The pre-judged condemnation of Henry Wirz has but one parallel in history. There are documents still in existence among the archives of England from the quaint hand of Thomas Cromwell, the infamous chancellor: "Ye Abbott Redyng must be sent down to be tryed and executed at Redyng"; and "You must send ye Abbott to Glaston to be tryed at Glaston and also to be executed there with his complycys; evydens to be well sortyd and endytments well drawn."

But once during the seventy-three consecutive days of the trial did Major Wirz show impatience and irritation. One day the witness, Gray, gave an extravagant piece of testimony that moved the commission. It was extremely damaging, and the prisoner sat up from his couch with clenched hands and as pale as death. Then he allowed his arms to fall by his side, and bowing his head he buried his face in his hands.

The scene was depicted and illustrated in the newspapers, as if Wirz had broken down in consciousness of his guilt.

The "important and reliable" witnesses for the prosecution were de la Baume, Gray, Spenas, Spring, Kellogg, Davidson, and a very few other lesser lights.

One of the disappointing witnesses from whom much was expected was the truthful Dr. A. W. Barrows. He was a physician before he enlisted, and was hospital steward of the Twenty-seventh Massachusetts Volunteers, and was afterward post-surgeon at a captured post in North Carolina. For some reason or other he had never received a commission. He entered Andersonville on May 28, and was there for nearly six months. Owing to his knowledge of medicine and his efficiency as a physician he was paroled by Captain Wirz, and took charge of one of the hospital departments.

His soul was too large to show ingratitude to the man who had favored and befriended him, and not a word derogatory to Captain Wirz could be wrung from him. He testified to the suffering and misery at Andersonville, and was detained as a witness but a few moments.

There were a few Confederate surgeons, hospital attendants, and guards that were subpoened by the Government, and who testified to conditions in and about the prison, but nothing as to cruelty on the part of the defendant.

The following letter in the original cut quite a figure at the trial:

"Andersonville, Sept. 17, 1864.

"Captain Wirz: You will permit Surgeon Jones, who has orders from the Surgeon-General, to visit the sick within the stockade that are under medical treatment. Surgeon Jones is ordered to make certain investigations which may prove useful to his profession.

"Very respectfully,

"W. S. WINDER, A. A. G.

"By order of Gen. Winder.

"Captain H. WIRZ, Commandant Prison."

At this distance this looks like an ordinary, harmless order, but in September and October, 1865, it was not viewed with so much complacency. It was read between the lines, and construed to mean something mysterious and dangerous in the

14

highest degree to the perpetuity of the Republic and the peace and dignity thereof.

Another letter was introduced in evidence that afforded considerable speculation, and this speculation had considerable bearing on the case, and all went to prove the presence of a "conspiracy." This piece of evidence was introduced for the purpose of showing the machinations and wicked designs of the "so-called" Southern Confederacy. Prosecutor Chipman in his closing address dwelt upon it to considerable length.

It was dated "Richmond, Va., August 6, 1864," and directed to "Dr. J. H. White, Surgeon in Charge of the Hospital for Federal Prisoners, Andersonville, Ga.":

"Sir: The field of pathological investigation afforded by the large collection of Federal prisoners in Georgia is of great extent and importance, and it is believed that results of value to the profession may be obtained by careful examination of the effects of disease upon a large body of men subjected to a decided change of climate and the circumstances peculiar to prison life. The surgeon in charge of the hospital for Federal prisoners, together with his assistants, will afford every facility to Surgeon Joseph Jones in the prosecution of the labors ordered by the Surgeon-General. The medical officers will assist in the performance of such post-mortems as Dr. Jones may indicate, in order that this great field for pathological investigation may be explored for the benefit of the Medical Department of the Confederate States Armies.

"S. P. MOORE,

"Surgeon-General."

The reader can read the above letter a dozen times without discovering anything diabolical in it, but the Military Commission thought otherwise. They could see "nothing good coming out of Nazareth."

In commenting on this significant letter, historian Ambrose Spencer in his "Narrative of Andersonville" (page 249) says:

"It is hard to conceive with what devilish malice, or criminal devotion to his profession, or reckless disregard of the high duties imposed upon him – I scarcely know which – he could sit down and deliberately pen such a letter of instructions as that given to Dr. Jones. Was it not enough to have cruelly starved and murdered our soldiers? Was it not enough to have sought to wipe out their very memories by burying them in nameless graves?"

The very sending of Dr. Jones to Andersonville by Surgeon-General Moore was a meritorious and commendable act!

I will give only a fragment, because it is enough, of Judge-Advocate Chipman's plea:

"Let us see what the evidences are of a common design to murder by starvation, these hapless, helpless wretches. First, the officers, high and low, civil and military, whom the evidence implicates in this great crime. As I have showed you by the testimony, there were associated in this conspiracy, as directly implicated and as perpetrators, the prisoner at the bar, Gen. John H. Winder, Surgeon Josiah H. White, Surgeon R. R. Stevenson, Dr. W. J. W. Kerr, Captain R. B. Winder, Captain W. S. Winder, Captain Reed, W. W. Turner, and Benjamin Harris. Remote from the scene, but no less responsible than those named – nay, rather with a greater weight of guilt resting upon them, are the leader of the rebellion, his war minister, his Surgeon-General, his Commissary and Quartermaster-General, his Commissioner of Exchange, and all others sufficiently high in authority to have prevented these atrocities, and to whom the knowledge of them was brought."

The testimony was all in and the case came to an end November 4, 1865.

The deliberations of the commission were brief and the following order was issued.

"General Court Martial; Order No. 607.

"War Department, Adjutant General's Office,

"Washington, D. C., November 6, 1865.

"Before a Military Commission which convened at Washington, D. C., August 23, 1865, pursuant to paragraph 3, Special Orders No. 453, dated August 23, 1865, and paragraph 13, Special Orders No. 524, dated October 2, 1865, War Department, Adjutant-General's Office, Washington, and of which Major-General Lewis Wallace, United States Volunteers, is president, was arraigned and tried Henry Wirz.

"FINDINGS – The Commission having maturely considered the evidence adduced, find the accused Henry Wirz as follows:

"Of the specifications to Charge I, Guilty after amending said specification to read as follows:

"In this, that the said Henry Wirz, did combine, confederate and conspire with them the said Jefferson Davis, James A. Seddon, Howell Cobb, John H. Winder, W. Shelby Reed, R. R. Stevenson, S. P. Moore, W. J. W. Kerr, James Duncan, Wesley W. Turner, Benjamin Harris, and others, whose names are unknown, citizens of the United States aforesaid, and who, were then engaged in armed rebellion against the United States, maliciously, traitorously, and in violation of the laws of war, to impair and injure the health and to destroy the lives, by subjecting to great torture and great suffering, by confining in unhealthy and unwholesome quarters, by exposing to the inclemency of winter and to the dews and burning sun of summer, by compelling the use of impure water, and by furnishing insufficient and unwholesome food, of a large number of Federal prisoners, to wit: forty-five thousand soldiers in the military service of the United States of America, held as prisoners of war at Andersonville, in the State of Georgia, within the lines of the so-called Confederate States, on or before the 27th day of March, 1864, and at divers times between that day and the tenth day of April, 1865, to the end, that the armies of the United States might be weakened and impaired, and the insurgents engaged in armed rebellion against the United States might be aided and comforted.

"Of charge I, *Guilty*.

"Of specification first to charge II, *Guilty*.

"Of specification second to charge II, *Guilty*.

"Of specification third to charge II, *Guilty*.

"Of specification fourth to charge II, *Not Guilty*.

"Of specification fifth to charge II, *Guilty*.

"Of specification sixth to charge II, *Guilty*.

"Of specification seventh to charge II, *Guilty*.

"Of specification eighth to charge II, *Guilty*.

"Of specification ninth to charge II, *Guilty*.

"Of specification tenth to charge II, *Guilty*.

"Of specification eleventh to charge II, *Guilty*.

"Of specification twelfth to charge II, *Guilty*.

"Of specification thirteenth to charge II, *Not Guilty*.

"Of charge II, *Guilty*.

"SENTENCE. – And the Commission does therefore sentence him, the said Henry Wirz, to be hanged by the neck till he be dead, at such time and place as the President of the United States may direct, two-thirds of the court concurring therein.

"SECOND. – The proceedings, findings, and sentence in the foregoing case having been submitted to the President of the United States the following are his orders:

" 'Executive Mansion,

" 'November 6th, 1865.

" 'The proceedings, findings, and sentence of the court in the within case are approved, and it is ordered that the sentence be carried into execution by the officer commanding the Department of Washington on Friday, the 10th day of November, 1865, between the hours of 6 o'clock A. M. and 12 o'clock noon.

" 'ANDREW JOHNSON,

" 'President.'

"THIRD. – Major-General C. C. Augur, commanding the Department of Washington, is commanded to cause the foregoing sentence in the case of Henry Wirz to be duly executed in accordance with the President's order.

"FOURTH. – The Military Commission, of which Major-General Lewis Wallace, United States Volunteers, is president, is hereby dissolved.

"By command of the President of the United States.

"E. D. TOWNSEND,
"Assistant Adjutant-General."

Thus ended the greatest judicial farce enacted since Oliver Cromwell, *et al.,* instituted the commission "to try and condemn" Charles I. The condemnation of Henry Wirz was the more pronounced outrage of the two, for the remains of Charles I were accorded something like a decent burial, whereas the body of Major Henry Wirz was consigned without ceremony to the prison-yard at Washington.

CHAPTER IV

THE LAST DAYS OF WIRZ'S LIFE

Permit me once more to revert to what I consider the most astonishing thing in connection with the trial of Major Wirz. The authorities spent three months in preparation before the trial (if it can be called a trial) began, and it lasted nearly three months, and yet of the thirteen prisoners that Wirz was charged with murdering on his own personal account, not the name of a victim was testified to and not a solitary one of them has been named since that time!

Think of it. Some of the prisoners lived three and four days after the alleged clubbing and shooting by Wirz, and one of the prisoners who was beaten, it was testified to by three or four witnesses, lived six days before he died, and notwithstanding thousands were in and about the prison no one could name them or knew who they were!

The dates of the alleged assaults, the facts down to the most minute particular were testified to with exactness, but in every case the most important thing – the name – was wanting.

After sentence was passed upon Wirz the authorities kindly allowed Attorney Schade to visit his unfortunate client. The meeting took place in the prisoner's cell, in the presence of an armed soldier.

Attorney Schade sat beside the prisoner and took his hand, and both wept, but of the two the soldier said that Schade was by far the more affected. The sympathetic and kind-hearted soldier, in speaking of it afterward, said that the scene was so affecting that he himself could not restrain his tears.

This man – "this monster" – whom I saw at Andersonville more than once melt into tears, while deploring the misery and suffering that he was unable to remedy, had now but four days to live. The sentence was no surprise to him nor to his patient, faithful, but powerless attorney.

The proceedings of the trial had hardly begun on the first day of the session, when Attorney Schade turned to his client and whispered, "You will be convicted," and the unfortunate victim slowly bowed his head in assent.

The next day after the interview with his attorney, Major Wirz being a Roman Catholic, requested permission to send for a priest of that faith. His jailors readily assented, and the Rev. F. E. Boyle waited upon Major Wirz in his cell. At the request of Father Boyle the soldier in attendance stepped one side.

Every movement and turn of the prisoner was reported and dilated upon and embellished by the press. Nothing was spoilt in the telling, and the fact that Major Wirz sent for a Roman Catholic priest was heralded throughout the country.

Some of the newspapers, striving to outstrip their contemporaries in journalistic enterprise, made indecent and insulting comments upon it. "The guilty monster wants to have his sins forgiven before he dies." "It will cost him a big sum for his shriving." "The first priest can name a big amount," said one, and at this time poor Wirz did not have a penny. Mr. Schade did not charge him for his service and he did not receive a cent from Wirz, because the poor, poverty-stricken prisoner did not have a cent to pay him.

Much was made over the fact that he had asked for a priest. This was a marked acknowledgment that he was guilty, or why should he send for a confessor?

It is well known, or ought to be well known, that every Roman Catholic about to die or when very sick sends for a priest. In that church there is a sacrament known as extreme unction, "the last rites of the church," and every member tries to avail himself of that rite. It is a universal custom in the Catholic church.

Even those philanthropic women whom Henry Ward Beecher, in a lecture delivered in 1865 or 1866, while speaking of the services of the Catholic "Sisters" on the field of battle and in the hospitals called "Human Angels," will call for a priest when about to die.

At this time Jefferson Davis, President of the

"so-called" Southern Confederacy, was in prison under indictment, and Lee and Johnston, owing to the terms agreed upon by Grant and Sherman, were free.

Louis Schade until he died always asserted that emissaries waited on him a few days before Wirz's execution and assured him that if the condemned man would implicate Jefferson Davis in the murders (?) at Andersonville that the sentence of Wirz would be commuted.

For more than forty years this statement has been discredited in the North and stigmatized as something worse than a wild romance. No credit whatever is attached to the late Attorney Louis Schade's voluntary statement. It is regarded as a falsehood pure and simple. As to the truth or falsity of the statement I know nothing; but let us briefly consider the evidence on that head for what it is worth.

Louis Schade said that the same statement was made to Father Boyle. The following is a copy of a letter written by Father Boyle to Jefferson Davis:

"Washington, D. C., October 10, 1880.

"Hon. JEFFERSON DAVIS.

"DEAR SIR: Absence from the city and the desire since my return to obtain information on the subject of your letter have delayed my answer. I have not succeeded in the latter purpose. But I know that on the evening before the day of the execution of Major Wirz a man visited me, on the part of a Cabinet officer, to inform me that Major Wirz would be pardoned if he would implicate Jefferson Davis in the cruelties at Andersonville. No names were given by this emissary, and upon my refusing to take any action in the matter he went to Mr. Louis Schade, counsel for Major Wirz, with the same purpose and with a like result.

"When I visited Major Wirz the next morning he told me that the same proposal had been made to him and had been rejected with scorn. The Major was very indignant, and said that, while he was innocent of the charges for which he was about to suffer death, he would not purchase his liberty by perjury and a crime such as was made the condition of his freedom.

"I attended the Major to the scaffold, and he died in the peace of God and praying for his enemies. I know that he was indeed innocent of all the cruel charges on which his life was sworn away, and I was edified by the Christian spirit in which he submitted to his persecutors.

"Yours very truly,

"F. E. BOYLE."

It is well known that it was the firm belief in the North at this time that Mr. Davis was more guilty than Major Wirz, and an effort was made to establish that fact. I have faith in Father Boyle's written statement. Not alone because he was a clergyman, but because he had no object in making the statement were it not true.

I am not a Roman Catholic. I am a Protestant, and come from Protestant stock as far back as can be traced; but knowing Major Wirz as well as I did, I would believe any statement that he would make two hours before his death.

I was confident that Major Wirz was innocent of the terrible charges of which he was condemned and that Father Boyle stated a fact in his letter to Jefferson Davis when he wrote, "I knew that he was indeed innocent of the cruel charges on which he was about to suffer death."

A venerable priest, Father Whelan, pastor of a Roman Catholic church at Savannah, Georgia, like the good Father Hamilton, often visited the prison at Andersonville to call on the sick.

The *Confederate Veteran* magazine, published at Nashville, Tennessee, in its March number, 1907, says:

"When Captain Wirz was under trial, Father Whelan went to Washington as a witness. He said that upon his arrival the prosecuting attorney asked him what he knew about the case; and after he had told all his observations at the prison, he was informed that he was not further wanted and could go home. Col. Robert Ould was another of the witnesses for the defense who were dismissed by the prosecution without being allowed to testify. Colonel Ould wrote:

" 'I was named by poor Wirz as a witness in his behalf. The summons was issued by Chipman, the judge-advocate of the military court. I obeyed the summons, and was in attendance upon the court for some ten days. The investigation had taken a wide range as to the conduct of the Confederate and Federal governments in the matter of the treatment of prisoners, and I thought the time had come when I could put before the world these humane offers of the Confederate authorities and the manner in which they had been treated. I so expressed myself more than once – perhaps too publicly. But it was a vain thought.

" 'Early in the morning of the day on which I expected to give my testimony I received a note requiring me to surrender my subpoena. I refused, as it was my protection in Washington. Without it the doors of the Old Capitol Prison might have opened and closed upon me. I engaged, however, to appear before the court, and I did so the same morning. I still refused to surrender my subpoena, and thereupon the judge-advocate indorsed upon it these words: "The within subpoena is hereby revoked; the person named is discharged from further attendance." ' "

I do not produce the above and similar statements from Southern sources for the purpose of reflecting upon Judge-Advocate Chipman or the military court that convicted Wirz, but to show that the temper of the times at that period in our history was such that no statement from our late enemies would be credited.

That Father Whelan and Colonel Ould were in attendance at the trial as witnesses but did not testify is a historical fact.

On the morning of November 10, 1865, a few hours before he mounted the scaffold, Major Wirz penned the following pathetic letter to his faithful friend and counsel:

"Old Capitol Prison,
"Washington, D. C., November 10, 1865.

"Dear Mr. LOUIS SCHADE:

"It is the last time that I address myself to you. What I have said often and often I repeat – accept my thanks, my sincere, heartful thanks, for all you have done for me. May God reward you. I cannot.

"I still have something more to ask of you, and I am confident you will not refuse to receive my dying request. Please help my poor family, my dear wife and children. War, cruelest, has swept everything from me, and to-day my wife and children are beggars!

"My life is demanded as an atonement. I am willing to give it, and hope that after a while I will be judged differently from what I am now. If any one ought to come to the relief of my family, it is the people of the South, for whose sake

I have sacrificed all. I know you will excuse me for troubling you again.

"Farewell, dear sir. May, God bless you.

"Yours thankfully,

"H. WIRZ."

No history of Andersonville written contains a word of the following touching letter sent by Major Wirz four days before his execution to President Andrew Johnson:

"Old Capitol Prison,

"November 6, 1865.

MR. PRESIDENT: With a trembling hand, with a heart filled with the most conflicting emotions, and with a spirit hopeful one moment and despairing the next, I have taken the liberty of addressing you. When I consider your exalted position, when I think for a moment that in your hands rests the weal or woe of millions – yea, the peace of the world – well may I pause to call to my aid courage enough to lay before you my humble petition. I have heard you spoken of as a man willing and ready at all times and under all circumstances to do justice, and that no man, however humble he may be, need fear to approach you; and therefore, I have come to the conclusion that you will allow me the same privilege as extended to hundreds and thousands of others. It is not my desire nor intention to enter into an argument as to the merits of

15

my case. In your hands, if I am rightfully informed, are all the records and evidences bearing upon this point, and it would be presumption on my part to say one word about it. There is only one thing that I ask, and it is expressed in a few words: 'Pass your sentence.'

"For six weary months I have been a prisoner; for six months my name has been in the mouth of every one; by thousands I am considered a monster of cruelty, a wretch that ought not to pollute the earth any longer. Truly, when I pass in my mind over the testimony given, I sometimes almost doubt my own existence, I doubt that I am the Captain Wirz spoken of. I doubt that such a man as he is said to be ever lived, and I am inclined to call on the mountains to fall upon and bury me and my shame. But O, sir, while I wring my hands in mute and hopeless despair, there speaks a small but unmistakable voice within me that says, 'Console thyself; thou knowest thy innocence. Fear not; if men hold thee guilty, God does not, and a new life will pervade your being.' Such has been the state of my mind for weeks and months, and no punishment that human ingenuity can inflict could increase my distress.

"The pangs of death are short, and therefore I humbly pray that you will pass your sentence without delay. Give me death or liberty. The one I do not fear; the other I crave. If you believe me guilty of the terrible charges that have been heaped upon me, deliver me to the executioner. If not guilty in your estimation, restore me to liberty and life. A life as I am now living is no life. I breathe, sleep, eat; but it is only the mechanical functions I perform, and nothing more. Whatever you decide, I shall accept. If condemned to death, I shall suffer without a murmur. If restored to liberty I will thank and bless you for it.

"I would not convey the idea to your mind, Mr. President, that I court death. Life is sweet; however lowly or humble a man's station may be, he clings to life. His soul is filled with awe when he contemplates the future, the unknown land where judgment is before which he will have to give an account of his words, thoughts, and deeds. Well may I remember, too, that I have erred like all other human beings. But of those things for which I may perhaps suffer a violent death I am not guilty, and God judge me. I have said all that I wished to say. Excuse my boldness in addressing you, but I could not help it. I cannot bear this suspense much longer. May God bless you and be with you ! Yoar task is a great and fearful one. In life or death I shall pray for you and for the prosperity of the country in which I have passed some of my happiest as well as darkest days.

"Very respectfully,

"H. Wirz."

The late Attorney Schade said that this letter was ignored. No reply was made to it.

On the morning of November 10, Major Henry

Wirz received the last rites of his church. He told Father Boyle that he forgave his enemies. He made his peace with God, and when the officer who had charge of the execution came to notify him that the time had come, Wirz responded, "I am ready, sir," and in company with the officer, guard, and Father Boyle, mounted the steps leading to the scaffold. He met his death without a tremor, like the brave man that he *was*.

Shortly after her husband was placed in the Washington prison, Mrs. Wirz came to Washington City and remained there several weeks. She rarely had an opportunity to meet her husband or converse with him.

During the time that she was in Washington her brother, who resided at Cadiz, Kentucky, went to Georgia and returned to his home with Major Wirz's little ten-year-old daughter and her two sisters, the daughters of Mrs. Wirz by a former marriage.

Shortly before the execution the final parting between Major Wirz and his wife took place in the prison, and the heart-broken woman returned to her children at the home of her brother.

Major Wirz was the object of that popular injustice that personifies causes and demands victims for unpopular movements. All the accumulated passions of the war were concentrated upon this one man. He was the magnet that drew the Northern wrath to satiety.

After his death the North drew a long breath

and began to think. The truth "crushed to earth" began slowly to rise, and the facts that had been suppressed at Washington relative to the non-exchange of prisoners became partially known. During the summer and fall of 1864 the understanding in the North was that the Southern Confederacy preferred to murder prisoners by starvation rather than exchange them. The North was slow to learn the falsity of this charge, but about the time of Major Wirz's death or soon after the scales began slowly to fall from Northern eyes.

During the trial of Major Wirz and at the time of his execution, Major R. B. Winder, the Confederate officer who was on duty at Andersonville and who was charged with Major Wirz as an accomplice in the conspiracy to starve and murder "Union prisoners," was shortly afterward liberated.

The revulsion of feeling in the North over the unjust execution of poor Wirz was too strong even for "the great War Secretary" to face, and Jefferson Davis, Alex. H. Stephens, General Cobb, Josiah H. White, R. R. Stevenson, W. J. W. Kerr, Captain Reed, and last but not least, Colonel Ould, the "Confederate Commissioner of Exchange," were never brought to trial! Therefore, poor ill-fated Wirz must have "conspired" single-handed and alone to starve and murder Union prisoners!

The attitude of the *New York News* regarding the trial and execution of Captain Wirz was strikingly in contrast to the Northern journals of the day.

In December, 1865, the News published a correspondence from Macon, Georgia, of which the following is an extract. I give it to show the feeling in the South at the time, and it is the same to-day:

"It has been some weeks since the trial of Captain Wirz, but it is not too late to say that his execution has produced a painful sensation throughout the Southern States. At the time of his arrest the people here knew but little of the commandant at Andersonville, and cared less; but subsequent developments, and especially the bloodthirsty disposition evinced by the Government of a great nation and the manly bearing of the prisoner on the scaffold, have made the whole Southern people mourners over his grave. They never believed him nor anybody else guilty of the crimes alleged against him. They knew it was impossible for such crimes to be committed without their knowledge. They knew more – that the people of these much-abused and much-wronged States are incapable of such barbarities. When, therefore, Captain Wirz, standing under the gallows and on the very brink of the grave, declared his innocence, they believed he spoke the truth.

"This is not all. They believed that Stanton wanted to treat the populace at the North to a bloody spectacle; they believed he wanted to divert attention from his own barbarous and persistent refusal to exchange prisoners of war; they believed he deliberately resolved to make poor Wirz the scapegoat of the iniquities of his own Government and of himself, and to this end he violated the spirit and the letter of the military convention between Johnston and Sherman as well as the fundamental law of the land. They believed, moreover, that the military commission before which Wirz was tried, setting aside all decency and catching at the spirit of the Secretary of War, was overbearing and dictatorial, and that he did not have a fair trial. And, finally, they believed the war minister of the Government, taking counsel of his passions, his prejudices, and his hatreds, sought by the conviction and execution cf Wirz to write a false chapter in the history of the war and to infamize the South.

"No one knows so well as the Secretary of War how much foundation there is for this belief. That there is some foundation for it is proved by the following truthful statement: One of the most truthful and reliable men in Georgia, an eminent surgeon, was summoned to Washington as a witness for the prosecution. Supposing the judge-advocate was desirous only of getting the truth he went to him before he was put on the stand and stated to him that the vaccine matter used upon the prisoners at Andersonville was introduced into the South from abroad, and was used upon the women and children in the country just as it was at the prison and with precisely the same effect, until it was discovered to be deleterious. This statement was made to disabuse the mind of the judge-advocate of the impression that an unfit article of vaccine matter had been used upon the prisoners for the purpose of destroying them. And yet the judge-advocate failed to interrogate the witness upon this point when he put him on the stand! Nay, more; when the witness was subsequently recalled by the defense and asked to explain this matter, the judge-advocate used all his legal ingenuity to prevent the truth coming out!

"But further: A returned prisoner had testified to a chapter of horror at Andersonville. Upon descending from the stand and being accosted by an acquaintance in the lobby, he remarked in the hearing of the surgeon alluded to above that what he had just sworn to 'was all a d— lie'; and that others had been telling big lies, and he thought he would see if he could not beat them all; and if the defense would secure him against a prosecution, he would return to the stand and swear it all away.

"Captain Wirz seemed solicitous in his parting interview with Captain Winder about his future reputation. His uneasiness was groundless, so far as the South is concerned. He is already regarded as the victim of a conspiracy against the truth of history – a martyr, who met his fate with a grace and heroism that has never been excelled. How much good such an execution will accomplish in restoring friendly feeling to the people of the two sections and connecting the torn and blood-stained Union remains to be seen. The military gentlemen who composed the commission, with Mr. Stanton at their back, have had their fleeting triumph. Wirz will have his in history. The day will yet come when they will deplore the parts they played in this disreputable tragedy. The truth cannot be always hid under a bushel. The radical conspirators against history may have the ear of the world just now, but sooner or later the truth will come out. 'The eternal years of God are hers.' The followers of Davis, Lee, and Jackson can bide their time, remembering what the great poet of Israel said: 'I have seen the wicked in great power, and spreading himself like a green bay tree; yet he passed away, and lo! he is not.' "

CHAPTER V

WIRZ'S ATTORNEY'S FINAL WORD

The following letter, which appeared in a Washington, D. C., newspaper, was addressed to the American public and was written by Captain Wirz's attorney:

"Washington, D. C.,
"April 4, 1867.

"To the American Public:

"Intending to leave the United States, I feel it my duty before I start to fulfill a promise which, a few hours before his death, I gave to my unfortunate client, Captain Henry Wirz, who was executed at Washington on the 10th of November, 1865. Protesting up to the last moment his innocence of those monstrous crimes with which he was charged, he received my word that, having failed to save him from a felon's doom, I would as long as I lived do everything in my power to clear his memory. I did that the more readily, as I was then already convinced that he suffered wrongfully. Since that time his unfortunate children, both here and in Europe, have constantly implored me to wipe out the terrible stains which now cover the name of their father.

"Though the times do not seem propitious for

obtaining justice, yet, considering that man is mortal, I will, before entering upon a perilous voyage, perform my duty to, those innocent orphans and also to myself. I will now give a brief statement of the causes which led to the arrest and execution of Captain Wirz.

"In April, 1865, President Johnson issued a proclamation stating that from evidence in the possession of the Bureau of Military Justice it appeared that Jefferson Davis was implicated in the assassination of Abraham Lincoln, and for that reason the President offered one hundred thousand dollars for the capture of the then fugitive ex-President of the Southern Confederacy. That testimony has since been found to be entirely false and a mere fabrication, and the suborner, Conover, is now under sentence in the jail in this city, the two perjurers whom he suborned having turned state's evidence against him; whilst the individual by whom Conover was suborned has not yet been brought to justice.

"Certain high and influential enemies of Jefferson Davis, either then already aware of the character of the testimony of those witnesses, or not thinking their testimony quite sufficient to hang Mr. Davis, expected to find the wanting material in the terrible mortality of Union prisoners at Andersonville.

"Orders were issued accordingly to arrest a subaltern officer, Captain Wirz, a poor, friendless, and wounded prisoner of war (he being included in the surrender of General Johnston) and besides, a foreigner by birth. On the ninth of May he was placed in the Old Capitol prison at Washington, and from that time the greater part of the Northern press was busily engaged in forming the unfortunate man in the eyes of the Northern people into such a monster that it became almost impossible to obtain counsel; even his countryman, the Swiss Consul-General, publicly refused to accept money to defray the expenses of the trial. He was doomed before he was heard, and *even the permission to be heard according to law was denied him.*

"To increase the excitement and give eclat to the proceeding and to influence still more the public mind the trial took place under the very dome of the Capitol of the nation.

"A military commission, presided over by a despotic general, was formed, and the paroled prisoner of war, his wounds still open, was so feeble that he had to recline during the trial on a sofa. *How that* trial *was conducted the whole world knows!*

"The enemies of generosity and humanity believed it to be a sure thing to get at Jefferson Davis, therefore the first charge was that of conspiracy between Henry Wirz, Jefferson Davis, Howell Cobb, R. B. Winder, R. R. Stevenson, W. J. W. Kerr, and a number of others *to kill the Union prisoners.*

"The trial lasted for three months; but fortun-

ately for the blood-thirsty instigators, not a particle of evidence was produced showing the existence of such a conspiracy; yet *Captain Wirz was
found guilty of that charge!*

"Having thus failed, another effort was made.
On the night before the execution of the prisoner
(November 9, 1865) a telegram was sent to the
Northern press from this city, stating that Wirz
had made important disclosures to General L. C.
Baker, the well-known detective, implicating Jefferson Davis, and that the confession would probably be given to the public. On the same evening some parties came to the confession of Wirz,
Rev. Father Boyle, *and also to me,* one of them in-
forming me that a high Cabinet official wished to
assure Wirz that if he would implicate Jefferson
Davis with the atrocities committed at Andersonville, his sentence would be commuted. The mes-
senger requested me to inform Wirz of this. In
the presence of Father Boyle, I told Wirz next
morning what had happened.

"The Captain simply and quietly replied, 'Mr.
Schade, you know that I have always told you that
I do not know anything about Jefferson Davis.
He had no connection with me as to what was done
at Andersonville. If I knew anything about him,
I would not become a traitor against him or any-
body else even to save my life.'

"He likewise denied that he had ever made any
statement to General Baker. Thus ended the attempt to suborn Captain Wirz against Jefferson

Davis. That alone shows what a man he was. Hom many of his defamers would have done the same? With his wounded arm in a sling, the poor paroled prisoner mounted the scaffold two hours later. His last words were that he died innocent, and so he did.

"The 10th of November, 1865, will indeed be a black stain upon the pages of American history.

"To weaken the effect of his declaration of innocence and of the noble manner in which Wirz died, a telegram was manufactured here and sent North stating that on the 27th of October, Mrs. Wirz (who actually on that day was nine hundred miles from Washington) had been prevented by that Stantonian *deus ex machina,* General L. C. Baker, *from poisoning her husband.* Thus at the time when the unfortunate family lost their husband and father, a cowardly and atrocious attempt was made to blacken their character also. On the next day I branded the whole as a lie, and since then I have never heard of it again, though it emanated from a brigadier-general of the United States Army.

"All those who were charged with having conspired with Captain Wirz have since been released, except Jefferson Davis. Captain Winder was let off without trial; and if any of the others have been tried, which I do not know, certainly not one of them has been hanged. As Captain Wirz could not conspire alone, nobody will now, in view of that important fact, consider him guilty of that charge.

"As to 'murder in violation of the laws and customs of war,' I do not hesitate to assert that about one hundred and forty-five out of one hundred and sixty witnesses that testified on both sides, declared during the trial *that Captain Wirz never murdered or killed any Union prisoners with his own hands or otherwise.*

"Those witnesses, some twelve or fifteen, who testified that they saw Wirz kill prisoners with his own hands or otherwise, swore falsely, abundant proof of that assertion being in existence. The hands of Captain Henry Wirz are clear of the blood of prisoners of war. He would certainly have at least intimated to me a knowledge of the alleged murders with which he was charged. No names of the alleged murdered men could be given, and when it was done no such prisoner could be found or identified.

"The terrible scene in court when he was confronted with one of the witnesses, and the latter insisting that Wirz was the man who killed a certain Union prisoner which irritated Wirz so much that he nearly fainted, will still be remembered. That witness, Gray, swore falsely, and God alone knows what the poor innocent prisoner must have suffered at that moment. The scene was depicted and illustrated in the Northern newspapers as if Wirz had broken down on account of his guilt.

Seldom has a mortal man suffered more than that friendless and forsaken man.

"But who is responsible for the many lives that were lost at Andersonville and in the Southern prisons? That question has not fully been settled, but history will yet tell on whose heads the guilt for those sacrificed hecatombs of human beings is to be placed. It was certainly not the fault of poor Wirz, when in consequence of medicines being declared contraband of war by the North, the Union prisoners died for the want of the same. How often have we read during the war that ladies going South had been arrested and placed in the Old Capitol Prison by the Union authorities, because genuine and other medicine had been found in their clothing! Our Navy prevented the ingress of medical stores from the seaside and our troops repeatedly destroyed drug stores and even the supplies of private physicians in the South.

"Thus the scarcity of medicine became general all over the South.

"That provisions in the South were scarce will astonish nobody, when it is remembered how the war was carried on. General Sheridan boasted in his report that in the Shenandoah Valley alone he burned more than two thousand barns filled with wheat and corn and all the mills in the whole tract of country; that he destroyed all factories and killed or drove off every animal, even poultry, that could contribute to human sustenance. And these desolations were repeated in different parts of the

South, and so thoroughly that money had to be appropriated to keep the people from starving. The destruction of railroads and other means of transportation by which food could be supplied by abundant districts to those without it increased the difficulties in giving sufficient food to our prisoners.

"The Confederate authorities, aware of their inability to maintain the prisoners, informed the Northern agents of the great mortality, and urgently requested that the prisoners should be exchanged, even without regard to the surplus, which the Confederates had on the exchange roll from former exchanges – that is, man for man. But our War Department did not consent to an exchange. They did not want to 'exchange skeletons for healthy men.'

"Finally, when all hopes for exchange were gone, Colonel Ould, the Confederate Commissioner of Exchange, offered early in August, 1864, *to deliver up all sick and wounded* without requiring an equivalent in return, and pledged that the number would amount to ten or fifteen thousand, and if it did not he would make up either number by adding well men. Although this offer was made in August, the transportation was not sent for them until December, although he urged that haste be made. During that very period most of the deaths occurred. It might be well to inquire

15

who these 'skeletons' were that Secretary of War Stanton did not want to exchange for healthy men.

"A noble and brave soldier never permits his antagonist to be calumniated and trampled upon after an honorable surrender. Besides, notwithstanding the decision of the highest legal tribunal in the land that military commissions are unconstitutional, and earnest and able protestations of President Johnson and the results of military commissions, yet such military commissions are again established by recent legislation of Congress all over the suffering and starving South. History is just, and, as Mr. Lincoln used to say, 'We cannot escape history.' Puritanical hypocrisy, self-adulation, and self-glorification will not save the enemies of liberty from their just punishment.

"Not even Christian burial of the remains of Captain Wirz has been allowed by Secretary Stanton. They still lie side by side with those of another and acknowledged victim of military commissions, the unfortunate Mrs. Surratt, in the yard of the former jail of this city.

"If anybody should desire to reply to this, I politely beg that it may be done before the first of May next, as I shall leave the country – but to return in the fall. After that day letters will reach me in care of the American Legation or Mr. Benedete Bobzani, Leipsig Street, No. 38, Berlin, Prussia.

"LOUIS SCHADE,
"Attorney at Law."

CHAPTER VI

THE GREAT WAR SECRETARY

Edwin McMasters Stanton was born in Ohio, December 19, 1814, and graduated at Kenyon College in 1833, and was soon after admitted to the bar. Near the end of Buchanan's administration, Stanton was called to act as Attorney-General. In 1862 President Lincoln had great difficulties with his war office, and notwithstanding Stanton had always been a Democrat he was appointed Secretary of War. It was like home to him. His intense vigor, unbounded power of organization, indomitable will, and unflagging industry constituted the principal traits of the great War Secretary.

He was not slow in letting the politicians, the generals, and the public know that he was the Secretary of War.

It has been conceded even by his enemies that the times, required a Stanton.

He was brave, blunt, honest, and outspoken. His quarrels with McClellan, Meade, Grant, and Sherman prove this. Lincoln was too great to quarrel with him and Grant appeared to be the only man with whom he came in contact that didn't fear him. "I'll fight it out on this line if it takes all summer," was Grant's response to repeated orders to advance.

Halleck quailed before him.

Stanton's obsequioas biographer is forced to admit, "It was not easy for his associates to get on with him comfortably."

An Illinois colonel conspicuously distinguished himself in one of the early battles and was promoted brigadier-general. Secretary Stanton was not consulted and knew nothing about it until after the promotion. The brigadier was a well-known friend of the President's, and soon after receiving his commission he visited Washington. He called upon Lincoln and afterward called at the War Department.

"Mr. Secretary," said he, "I took a run into the city for a few days' rest and called to pay my respects."

"You get back to your brigade at once," roared Stanton. "If you remain in Washington another day, I'll have you court-martialed."

There was nothing of the trimmer about Secretary Stanton, nor the ways of the politician. Hypocrisy had no place in his make-up. He was thoroughly incorrupt and incorrigibly honest. After living through boundless opportunities of peculation, he was so poor when he died that his library had to be sold to defray his funeral expenses.

In 1866 and 1867 he waged a bitter war with President Johnson. He refused to be removed from the War Department. His fight with the President was a battle of the giants, and during the impeachment proceedings he took 'an active part, and on the acquittal of Johnson he resigned and resumed the practice of law. In 1859 President Grant made him a justice of the Supreme Court; but his mighty work during the trying war times had worn him out, and he died December 24, 1869.

His was a singular character. That he was a man of unswerving integrity, of unbounded patriotism, honesty of purpose, and a man of great executive ability, none will deny; but that his course relative to the non-exchange of prisoners was extremely cruel and cold-blooded, all must confess.

I love my country – my *whole* country, and was no more loyal to the perpetuity of the Union in 1861 than I am to-day, but I have come to the conclusion that after forty years we can at least afford to tell the truth.

For more than forty years we of the North have been acting unfairly. We charge the South with all the blame for all the horrors of the Civil War. We pensioners of the Union Army accept without thanks the assessments from the old Confederate taxpayer, but when he suggests the erection of a monument to the brave but unfortunate victims of the war, we raise our hands in holy horror and protest, while at the same time we are contemplating building a monument to John Brown at Harper's Ferry, or at Washington.

We profess unstinted friendship toward the South, and we are anxious that amity and good feeling between all sections of our common country shall prevail and that all the bitterness of war feeling shall be obliterated forever. Let us be honest and sincere and prove it by asking Congress to enact a law granting a pension to our brave, mistaken brother, the maimed and forgiven Confederate soldier. This will never be done, but there is logic and equity in the thought. The Southern taxpayer cheerfully contributes his share toward the national pension appropriation.

When this takes place it will be living testimony of our protestation of good feeling, amity, and friendship, and it will also be evidence that we are one great, patriotic, indissoluble nation.

I beg to remind the critic that censures me for this broad statement, that the Confederate veteran is not a foreigner. He is our brother, he is related to us by the closest blood ties, and he is our countryman. He was mistaken, but for that mistake is there even now at this late day no forgiveness? *Politics* is the only thing in the way to-day preventing our Government from coming to his aid in his declining years.

To my ex-prisoner comrades who differ with me and still insist that Captain Wirz was guilty and merited his tragic death, I would ask, Do you know of your own knowledge that he ever maimed

or killed a Union prisoner of war? Isn't it prejudice, pure and simple, prejudice caused by your
privations and suffering at Andersonville? Does
not that memory cause your judgment to be
warped? I judge Henry Wirz from my personal
knowledge of his character. Let us be fair and
"place ourselves in the other fellow's place."
Would you or could you have done better if you
had been in his place under the same circumstances?

And lastly it may be said that I have aired my
sentiments too freely and in doing so have been dis-
loyal to the North and that I have been over-cen-
sorious of my country. I deny it. The South is
as much my country as the North. I love and
revere the whole land from ocean to ocean, and
from the St. Lawrence to the Gulf. In my humble
capacity I have completed a work that I have
been contemplating for many years. I have no
apology to make except it is that I could wish some
abler pen than mine had undertaken it – the vindi-
cation of an unfortunate and much-wronged man,
who was the victim of the times in which he lived.
I have touched on other matters, it is true, but was
obliged to do so in consequence of the needs of my
story, and to portray the temper of the times. I
was obliged to handle some matters without
gloves, and in doing so may have offended.

We who have fought during the Civil War for
the perpetuity of the Union can testify to the
Spartan-like bravery of those who then confronted

us, but who are to-day our countrymen and our brothers. The sectional bitterness, thank God, has disappeared, and let us of the North be honest and manly enough to concede facts.

The man in gray was sincere in his convictions. He loved his sunny Southland, and no Greek at Thermopylae or Marathon fought more valorously for his home and little ones than did the Southern soldier on many a battlefield. He was vanquished and, "turning his back on the battlefield, heavy-hearted, enfeebled by want and wounds, his money worthless, he sought his desolate home to begin life anew." We came marching home with "proud and glorious tread," glad that the cruel war was over, and were welcomed with loud acclaim by our friends and amid the cheers of a grateful nation. What a contrast!

The loyalty, heroism, devotion, and suffering of the women of the South have never been fully told and never will be fully known.

Nothing I ever experienced gave me so much pleasure as did the sight of our National emblem on the public buildings in the large cities, in the South, on my visit there a few years ago. I had not been there since I was discharged in 1865, and the change was great. I felt then as I do now, that every American citizen should thank God that we are one people, one country under one flag.

Then let us wipe out the so-called "Mason and Dixon's line," and hang out the latch-string for each other.

 Bringing the Past into the Future
More Great Books Brought Back by DSI

Series 1: Lincoln
Special Series 1 includes a total of nine volumes: *The Life of Abraham Lincoln* by Ida Tarbell, a four-volume set; *Debates of Lincoln and Douglas; Six Months at the White House with Lincoln* by F. B. Carpenter; and *Herndon's Lincoln: The True Story of a Great Life*, three volumes unabridged, written by Lincoln's law partner of more than twenty years.
CD-ROM ISBN 1-58218-084-9

The Life of Abraham Lincoln
By Ida M. Tarbell. Illustrations and maps. 4 vols. Originally published by the Lincoln Historical Society in 1900.
Discover the incredible facts of the life of Abraham Lincoln, a man who changed the fabric of America forever. Read in his own words his views on equality and ending slavery. This work details Lincoln's entire life including the origins of the Lincoln family, his entry into the military during the Black Hawk War, his important law cases, his entire political career, the Civil War, his personal life with Mary Todd, the devastating loss of one of their children, and his constant battles with depression.
CD-ROM ISBN 1-58218-017-2
Softcover ISBN 1-58218-002-4

Debates of Lincoln and Douglas
Carefully prepared by the reporters of each party at the times of their delivery. Originally published by Follett & Foster in 1860.
Perhaps the most consequential artifact of American election campaigning and its political arguments. Political debates between Hon. Abraham Lincoln and Hon. Stephen A. Douglas, in the celebrated campaign of 1858 in Illinois. Included are the preceding speeches of each at Chicago, Springfield, etc., as well as the two great speeches of Lincoln in Ohio in 1859, published at the times of their delivery.
CD-ROM ISBN 1-58218-009-1
Softcover ISBN 1-58218-000-8

Series 2: Custer
Special Series 2 includes both *A Life of Major Gen'l George A. Custer* by Frederick Whittaker and *Tenting on the Plains* by Custer's wife, Elizabeth. Also included are the National Archives' transcripts concerning the Court Martial of Custer (1867) and the Court of Inquiry of Reno (1879) for his actions at Little Big Horn.
CD-ROM ISBN 1-58218-081-4

A Life of Major Gen'l George A. Custer
By Frederick Whittaker. Originally published in 1876.
With no marked advantages of education or wealth to command his situation, Custer yet passed through a career so brilliant that his deeds are household words, his "Last Stand" against Sioux and Cheyenne warriors at Little Big Horn an enduring legend in American history. Truth and sincerity, honor and bravery, tenderness and sympathy, unassuming piety and temperance were the mainspring of Major Gen'l Custer, the man.
CD-ROM ISBN 1-58218-042-3
Softcover ISBN 1-58218-040-7

Tenting on the Plains
By Elizabeth Custer. Includes illustrations by Frederic Remington. Originally published in 1889.
Elizabeth Custer was just a young girl when she fell in love with one of the most controversial Indian fighters of the late 1800s, and barely a woman when she defied her father to marry him. She went on to earn literary fame as well as financial independence with her entertaining tales of frontier life as the wife of General George Custer. Her stories of life on the Plains are as colorful today as when they first appeared over a century ago.
CD-ROM ISBN 1-58218-052-0
Softcover ISBN 1-58218-050-4

Series 3: Generals
Special Series 3 includes *Personal Memoirs of U. S. Grant, Memoirs of General W. T. Sherman, Personal Memoirs of P. H. Sheridan,* and *McClellan's Own Story.*
CD-ROM ISBN 1-58218-082-2

Personal Memoirs of U. S. Grant
Illustrations, Maps, and Facsimiles of Handwriting. 2 vols. Originally published in 1885.
Published by Mark Twain under the Charles L. Webster Company imprint, this memoir is widely admired as one of the finest military autobiographies ever written. Grant recounts the failings and triumphs of his leadership in strong, clear prose including his boyhood in Ohio, his graduation from West Point, his marriage to Julia Dent, his brilliant military campaigns, and his presidency.
CD-ROM ISBN 1-58218-025-6
Softcover ISBN 1-58218-005-9

Memoirs of General W. T. Sherman
With a map showing the marches of U.S. forces under his command. 2 vols. Originally published in 1890.
General William Tecumseh Sherman, a great man both in his gifts and his achievements, was altogether a solider in his habits of mind. A natural student of the topography of the countryside, this characteristic of true military genius served Sherman well in planning his devastating march from Atlanta, across Georgia to the sea, the most striking achievement of the Civil War. The memoirs of this courageous, patient, and self-sacrificing "Old Warrior" are certain of a permanent place in literature.
CD-ROM ISBN 1-58218-025-3
Softcover ISBN 1-58218-004-0

Personal Memoirs of P. H. Sheridan
Illustrated. Twenty-six maps, prepared specially for this book by the War Department. 2 vols. Originally published in 1888.
General Phil Sheridan revolutionized the handling of mounted men in this country and abroad as commander of America's army. A hell-for-leather cavalryman, Sheridan was as deliberate and careful as he was brave. His memoirs vividly depict the brilliant campaigns he masterminded, including his victory at Appomattox where his men blocked Lee's retreat to force his surrender, ending the Civil War.
CD-ROM ISBN 1-58218-033-4
Softcover ISBN 1-58218-006-7

Digital Scanning, Inc. • 344 Gannett Road, Scituate, MA 02066 • www.digitalscanning.com • toll-free 1-838-349-4443

McClellan's Own Story
Illustrations from sketches drawn on the field of battle by A. R. Waud, the great war artist. Originally published in 1886.

After Bull Run, Lincoln appointed 34-year-old Gen. George B. McClellan as commander of the newly created Army of the Potomac. An able administrator and drillmaster, McClellan proceeded to reorganize the army for what he expected to be an overwhelming demonstration of Northern military superiority. "Our George," as his soldiers lovingly called him, was one of the ablest commanders which the United States has ever produced.
CD-ROM ISBN 1-58218-037-7
Softcover ISBN 1-58218-007-5

History of Massachusetts in the Civil War
By William Schouler, Late Adjutant-General of the Commonwealth. Originally published in 1868.

Massachusetts played a prominent part in the Civil War, from the beginning to the end; not only in furnishing soldiers for the army, sailors for the navy, and financial aid to the government, but in advancing ideas, which though scoffed at in the early months of the war, were afterwards accepted by the nation, before the war could be brought to a successful end.
CD-ROM ISBN 1-58218-013-X
Softcover ISBN 1-58218-001-6

Series 4: Indians
Special Series 4 includes George Catlin's *North American Indians* and *Indian Tribes of North America*. Also included are Indian Treaties from the National Archives.
CD-ROM ISBN 1-58218-083-0

North American Indians
By George Catlin. Illustrations and maps. 2 vols. Originally published in 1903.

Explore the territories of the North American Indian with the historical text, illustrations, and maps of George Catlin. Catlin gave up the practice of law to pursue his self-taught art, travelling throughout the American West from 1832 to 1840, painting portraits and writing on his encounters with various Indian tribes. Scholars and researchers alike will delight in the descriptions and portraits that portray this moment in history with such vivid detail.
CD-ROM ISBN 1-58218-021-0

Civil War Prison Stories

Daring and Suffering: A History of the Great Railroad Adventure
By Lieut. William Pittenger, One of Andrews' Raiders. Originally published in 1863.

This courageous raid into Georgia ranks high among the striking and novel incidents of the Civil War. Pittenger and his comrades embarked on a secret raid deep into Confederate territory to cut the rail link between Marietta and Chattanooga, only to run out of fuel after a long and dangerous chase. Those that survived the mission were the first soldiers at rank of private to be awarded the Congressional Medal of Honor.
CD-ROM ISBN 1-58218-077-6
Softcover ISBN 1-58218-075-X

Beyond the Lines: A Yankee Loose in Dixie
By Capt. J. J. Geer. Originally published in 1864.

Geer narrates the suffering endured as a prisoner in the Southern Confederacy. After being captured at the battle of Shiloh, Geer was tried on the most frivolous charges and subsequently chained with slaves' chains and cast into military prisons and common jails. He managed to escape, overcoming malarious marshes and bloodhounds only to be recaptured!
CD-ROM ISBN 1-58218-085-7
Softcover ISBN 1-58218-088-1

Prison Life in Dixie
By Sergeant Oats. Originally published in 1880.

The author describes his harrowing capture and imprisonment by the Rebels at Sumter Prison a.k.a. "Andersonville Prison Pen". Renowned as one of the worst prisons of the Civil War, the Andersonville pen spread over only 11 acres, with a 12-foot wall surrounding over 33,000 Union soldiers. The writer endeavors to furnish such descriptions and incidents that give the reader a true picture of Rebel prisons and the means and methods of either surviving or dying in them.
CD-ROM ISBN 1-58218-101-2
Softcover ISBN 1-58218-100-4

Forthcoming Titles

Herndon's Lincoln: The True Story of a Great Life
By William H. Herndon, Lincoln's friend and law partner

Six Months at the White House with Lincoln
By F. B. Carpenter

Reminiscences of Winfield Scott Hancock
By his wife, A. R. Hancock

The Battle of Gettysburg
By Comte de Paris

Sheridan's Troopers on the Border
By De B. Randolph Keim

Genesis of the Civil War
By Samuel Wylie Crawford

Following the Guidon
By Elizabeth Custer

The Indian Tribes of North America
By McKenney and Hall

The History of Philip's War
By Thomas Church

Book of the Indians of North America
By Samuel G. Drake

Digital Scanning, Inc. • 344 Gannett Road, Scituate, MA 02066 • www.digitalscanning.com • toll-free 1-888-349-4443

www.ingramcontent.com/pod-product-compliance
Lightning Source LLC
LaVergne TN
LVHW011219080426
835509LV00005B/223